# THE DIARY OF A BOMB AIMER

# THE DIARY OF A BOMB AIMER

CAMPBELL MUIRHEAD

SPELLMOUNT LTD

**In the Spellmount Military list:**

The Uniforms of the British Yeomanry Forces 1794–1914 Series:
*The Sussex Yeomanry*
*The North Somerset Yeomanry*
*The Yorkshire Hussars*
*Westmorland and Cumberland Yeomanry*
*3rd County of London (Sharpshooters)*
*Duke of Lancaster's Own Yeomanry*
*Yorkshire Dragoons*
*Lovat Scouts*

*The Yeomanry Regiments – A Pictorial history*
*Over the Rhine – The Last Days of War in Europe*
*Riflemen Form*
*History of the Cambridge University OTC*
*Yeoman Service*
*Intelligence Officer in the Peninsula*

**In the Nautical list:**

*Sea of Memories*

**In the Aviation list:**

*Diary of a Bomb Aimer*

First published in the UK 1987 by
Spellmount Ltd
12 Dene Way, Speldhurst
Tunbridge Wells, Kent TN3 0NX

ISBN 0-946771-75-8

**British Library Cataloguing in Publication Data**

Muirhead, Campbell
Diary of a bomb aimer
1. Great Britain, *Royal Air Force, Bomber Command* 2. World War, 1939–1945 – Aerial operations, British 3. World War, 1939–1945 – Personal narratives, British
I. Title
930.54'4941'0924 D786
ISBN 0-946771-75-8



Designed by Words & Images, Speldhurst, Tunbridge Wells, Kent.
Typeset by Vitaset, Paddock Wood, Kent.
Printed in Great Britain by Staples Printers Ltd, Rochester, Kent.

*TO ANN*

# FOREWORD

I think I have read almost every book about Bomber Command's activities in World War II. And thoroughly enjoyed – and been impressed by – all of them. But *Diary of a Bomb Aimer* by Campbell Muirhead, to use a modern phrase 'turned me on' more than any of them. I'm not sure I know the reason. Maybe it's because immediately a bombing raid was over he recorded the factual part of the operation starting with details of the bomb load, details of searchlights and night fighters, details of the actual bombing: and sometimes with reference to his own personal feelings about dropping bombs on women and children. We flew several times against the same targets, and, on three occasions dropped our bomb load within a minute of each other, which makes his diary personally interesting. Then, when not on operational flights, he recorded various facets of station life at RAF Wickenby and of personalities there. Also most interesting to read were his notes about his visits home to Edinburgh, the delightful Gresley Pacifics of the old LNER (plus a nostalgic reminder of the cost of a bottle of whisky then!) Next he's back from the relatively sane civilian world, recording his impressions of his next operational flight. In this respect I was surprised to read of his dislike of daylight raids over Occupied France and how he and his crew preferred to fly and to bomb under the cover of the night. Perhaps the more visible signs of violent defences had something to do with this, but for my part I would have been much more scared on that fiercely contested night attack on Brunswick which finished off his crew's tour of operations.

This book is, in my opinion, a very valuable piece of military history. Even down to the excerpts from the vulgar – and in some cases blasphemous – songs which Campbell Muirhead kept a note of in his little black book.

*Diary of a Bomb Aimer*, while of particular interest to those men and women, both aircrew and ground staff in the 60-odd age group who served in RAF Bomber Command in World War II (and of even more interest to the members of the Wickenby Register – an organisation of RAF personnel who have served at Wickenby) will also be of interest to the younger generation. Of that I am sure.

I am sure also that reading this Diary will cause some of those who belittle the damage caused to the German war machine by these Lancaster (and Halifax) bombers to reflect on the number of JU88s, ME110s and other Luftwaffe aircraft plus the thousands of 88mm and 105mm flack guns – all with personnel – which could have been diverted to the Eastern Front (with perhaps tipping the balance there in the tank battles) had it not been for RAF Bomber Command's dedication.

THE LORD SANDHURST, DFC
formerly Sandy Mansfield
Bombing Leader of 12 Squadron

# GLOSSARY

| | | |
|---|---|---|
| Op | : | Bombing operation over Occupied Europe or Germany |
| A/C (or a/c) | : | Aircraft |
| Flak | : | Enemy anti-aircraft fire |
| S/Ls | : | Searchlights |
| E/A | : | Enemy Aircraft |
| N/F | : | Nightfighters |
| Tit | : | Press-button on bombing toggle (to release bombs) |
| Kite | : | Aircraft |
| U/S | : | Unserviceable |

| | | |
|---|---|---|
| Commissioned ranks: | P/O: | Pilot Officer |
| | F/O: | Flying Officer |
| | F/L: | Flight Lieutenant |
| | W/C: | Wing Commander |
| Luftwaffe fighters: | JU 88: | Junkers 88 |
| | FW 190: | Focke Wulf 190 |
| | ME 109: | Messerschmitt 109 |
| | ME 110: | Messerschmitt 110 |

Plus, elsewhere, some RAF slang:–

| | | |
|---|---|---|
| ackers | : | money |
| (to) bind | : | to complain, make a nuisance of yourself |
| (the) bag | : | German POW camp |
| bod | : | a male person |
| brown job | : | soldier |
| (to) buy it | : | to be killed (or shot down) |
| chieffy | : | flight sergeant |
| clamped | : | non-flying weather |
| cock one up | : | salute |

**9 May 1944**
Arrived here today at No. 12 Squadron, No 1. Bomber Group, RAF Wickenby. From No. 1 Lancaster Flying School, Hemswell. There we converted from Halifaxes (our first 4-engined bomber; before that it was the 2-engined Wellington). As a crew we did six hours on Lancasters and were thereafter pronounced fit for posting to an operational flying unit. Six flaming hours only – they must be pretty desperate for operational air-crew!

Have decided to keep a diary of my operational flights and to this end have bought, in Woolworths, a little black notebook costing all of a tanner.

Might be a good idea also to enter up, now and then, something about the day-to-day life on an operational Squadron. If I have the time, that is.

**10 May 1944**
To be flying tonight. At 23:00hrs. A cross-country lasting just over 3 hours. That gives me enough time to do some more scribbling, but I think I'll note down the names and designations of our crew first:
Pilot – F/O Vernon
Bomb aimer – F/O Muirhead
Navigator – Sgt. Norman
Engineer – Sgt. Griggs
Wireless Operator – Sgt. Dunn
Mid-upper gunner – P/O Horsfall
Rear gunner – Sgt. Cartwright

Have ascertained two interesting, but somewhat chilling, facts since I arrived here. The first is that, while the operational tour consists of 30 flights over Germany and/or Occupied Europe, the chances of survival are said to be about 30 per cent. Now isn't that a cheerful and heart-warming note on which to get this diary under way . . .

The second is that 12 Squadron is no longer referred to as the (somewhat inevitable) 'Dirty Dozen'; it is referred to as the 'Chop Squadron'. Must find out more about this: hope it is in no way connected with current losses.

On entering the Mess for the first time, I was surprised to see, in the ante-room, an Austin Seven parked there on the carpet. A P/O told me that, actually, it belonged to his navigator. When I observed that the ante-room didn't seem the ideal parking place for a car he added that, well, his navigator didn't actually know it was there. Evidently his crew, who had done 20 ops, had been rewarded with 3 days' stand-down: his navigator, together with an oppo, had decided to take off for London: this oppo also had a car and they decided to save petrol by both going in his. The navigator's Austin Seven had therefore been left in a small parking space just outside the ante-room. Some bods decided that it was making the place look untidy: they measured the Mess outside door; also the door to the ante-room. They concluded that, if they unscrewed both doors from their supports, and removed certain parts of the Austin, they could just squeeze it in. Which they did. Once in, they put back the parts of the car they had removed. So there it stood in all its glory on the ante-room carpet. I noticed that somebody thoughtfully had placed a copy of *The Times* underneath the engine to protect the carpet from oil.

A couple of days later the car had vanished. Whether the original removal merchants had put their operation into reverse or whether the owner and cronies had removed it, I do not know.

Off to the Mess to eat now. Must say they feed you well here, the plentiful amount of food being excellently cooked and well presented. I think they must keep the best WAAF cooks for operational Squadrons.

**11 May 1944**

That cross-country was OK. We seem to work well together as a crew. Another one tonight: about 5 hours, take off 22:10hrs. Actually, we're not designated as being fully operational yet.

With most of the day off, I started researching this 'Chop Squadron' title. Apparently, it came about because of 12 Squadron's truly dreadful losses while part of the Advanced Air Striking Force in France and Belgium during 1940. They flew Battles, monoplane bombers with a maximum speed of 241mph at 13,000ft. and which could carry, over 1,050 miles, a bomb-load of only 1,000lbs. The armament of the Battle was pathetic; one Vickers Gas Operated .303 machine gun *fixed* in the port wing and another operated by the gunner on a Scarff mounting in his open cockpit. This against the ME109F which could do 355mph at 18,000ft. and was armed with 2x7.9 machine guns and 3x20mm cannon. Makes you want to weep. Also makes you even more contemptuous of the peace-at-any-price brigade who, between the wars, were at their most vociferous in proclaiming that the only way to ensure peace was to disarm. Well, maybe they didn't know then, but surely they know now. They must bear part of the responsibility in sending these obsolete aircraft against the ultra-modern Luftwaffe.

That's enough for today. Will return to this Battle business tomorrow.

**12 May 1944**

Getting a bit fed up with this: another stooge around tonight – the Flight Commander must think we're not quite ready for the real stuff. Really old Lancs on these training flights; certainly not the

Squadron's best. Which is understandable; the tip-top efforts must be kept for operations.

So I might as well finish off what I had started about the Battles. Evidently, on 10 May 1940, six Battles were to be despatched to bomb the concrete bridge at Vroenhoven over the Albert canal near Maastricht in a desperate attempt to delay the rapidly advancing Germans. All the crews were volunteers for what was virtually a suicide mission. Of the six, only five managed to get airborne. The cost of this operation was five losses out of five. That, together with an attack on the Sedan bridgehead on 14 May which cost the Squadron four out of five Battles, attracted, so I have learned, to No. 12 its grim distinction of being the 'Chop Squadron'. That noted, let's forget about it.

**13 May 1944**

Had just opened this wee black book when Vernon came in to announce we'd been granted seven days' leave. So off we go to collect passes and warrants. A bit of confusion there because the Orderly Room types hadn't been told to issue them. We send for the Adjutant. A bit of 'phoning, some apologising, and the documents are issued. We ask each other where they're going . Vernon's off to London, the sergeants to their home towns. Horsfall evidently has nowhere to go (he doesn't quantify this). So I ask him if he's ever been to Edinburgh. He says once and that he liked it. I invite him to come home with me to my folks' house which is at Portobello, three miles out of Edinburgh. He agrees and I promise to take him to most of the pubs in Rose Street.

**22 May 1944**

Arrived back today after a most enjoyable leave. Horsfall, I think, enjoyed himself too, though he doesn't say much about it.

**23 May 1944**

Airborne at 11:40 for a two hour air-test, then again at 16:35 for a 3½hr. stooge around. Boring.

Indications are that the weather's going to clamp down on us. Seems as if we're never going to get to that first one.

**28 May 1944**

And clamp it did. Until today. And guess what? Yes, yet another training flight. One thing about those training flights – every time you land, the Sally Ann seem to be around serving tea and buns from their little van. They never tire, these ladies. And they never try to shove religion down our throats. Equally, we watch our language in their presence. Which is a bit difficult as we swear so much.

One very interesting lecture a couple of days ago. By the Intelligence people. It was a long affair, but carried out informally with those who smoke doing so and everybody drinking tea. Sounds rather bumptious, but we knew most of it: but not all.

We knew, for instance, not to take our Forms 1250 (Identity Cards) with us on an op: not to have any letters on our person: not to have even the stub of a 'bus ticket lying unnoticed in a pocket. In fact, not to have anything on us apart from our identity discs. These come in their asbestos pair: asbestos because if you're burned to death the disc will still be around to prove it was you: and in a pair because one stays to keep your body company while the other is kept for reference purposes. Fatuous observations all around on 'discs, identity', with me, at least, mentally shrugging it all off and adopting this 'it couldn't happen to me and if it did I'd be beyond caring anyway' attitude.

But what we *didn't* know were the minute details of what happened to us if shot down, what we should do should this come about; and, more importantly, what we should not do.

Depended exactly where shot down for a start. If over France, you tried to contact the Resistance. No offence taken by the Intelligence types when asked, tongue-in-cheek, if you went around waving a placard with 'Wish to contact Resistance' across it. (Reckon they're used to this.) They explained how you'd try to hide yourself in the first instance and then attempt to contact the nearest priest: that the priest might wish to have nothing to do with you and might advise you to surrender to the nearest gendarme: that you were not to do so, but were to go into hiding again. Evidently all this because the Germans had been known to parachute their own men, dressed in RAF uniform, into Resistance areas during the course of an RAF night raid: these Germans contacted priests, were given shelter, were shepherded away by the Resistance: and when they decided that they had penetrated the network completely the trap was sprung and all the Resistance were rounded up and executed. Including the priest.

So, being rebuffed by the priest, into hiding you would go. Chances were that, being exhausted, you'd fall asleep. Equal chances were that you'd have a rude awakening; maybe by a slap across the face, maybe by a knife at your throat. Oh yes, the Resistance all right! But a deeply distrustful, deeply suspicious, Resistance. You were in for a rough time. All sorts of questions, including those about your home town. Then a wait while your answers were verified (from England, or so the Intelligence fellows said). Until then you'd be kept under close guard with the threat that one false move could see your throat slit. They made it sound so very dramatic – which I suppose it was meant to be.

Another thing we didn't know was that the RAF kept tabs on aircrew practically from the moment they went into the bag. We were told exactly where the Luftwaffe Reception Centre was. Also how long we'd be kept there before being transferred to a Stalagluft. They harped on and on about giving only name, rank and number; absolutely nothing else. The first Luftwaffe officer to interrogate you would in all probability be a hectoring bully full of threats about what would happen to you if you refused to give anything more than name, rank and number. At which stage our lecturer paused to await the virtually inevitable: 'What if they torture you?' 'Not,' he replied, 'if it's the Luftwaffe: they don't resort to torture or anything like that. But, if you get picked up by the Gestapo or the SS, well, that's a different matter.'

I felt like saying one would probably have little choice in the matter, that one could hardly say to the Gestapo or the SS thanks all the same but you'd rather hold on until the Luftwaffe turned up. Glad I didn't, because the chap went on to tell us that, in the event of the Gestapo or SS being first on the scene, the Luftwaffe weren't very far behind and that, Goering being second in line to Hitler and accordingly all-powerful, they would soon pluck you away from them.

He then returned to his theme re the bullying Luftwaffe type. He, he explained, would be followed by a charming, polished Luftwaffe officer who, in apologising for his colleague's loutish behaviour, would offer you cigarettes (Capstan, usually – the Germans picked up tens of thousands of them at Dunkirk) and murmur that this really wasn't an interrogation or anything like that, just a personal chat between two operational flying men. He was, by far, the more dangerous of the two. He might, for example, after a short while, suggest that, as an officer and a gentleman, if you'd give him your *parole* for 24hrs. he'd take you out for a drink; he'd maybe even add that he knew a couple of rather gorgeous girls who, their boyfriends (or husbands) being away at the front, were feeling rather frustrated. At this stage all humour departed from the Intelligence Officer's face: and his pace of delivery slowed to accentuate the gravity of his words. 'If he does this,' he intoned, 'It's because you've told him *more* than just your name, rank and number: you've told him enough to make him feel you're worth working on. And, be in no doubt about it, we back here will know about it. If you're at that Centre more than two weeks before being despatched to your Stalagluft a little mark will go against your name and we'll want a word with you after the war': and he gave us the names of certain individuals at certain camps of whom we were to be very suspicious indeed. He also warned us that, in no circumstances were we to complete a so-called Red Cross form which, he said, was completely bogus.

Personally, I felt the Intelligence types, over at least some of the foregoing, were laying it on somewhat. Hope like hell I never have the chance to prove whether they were, or were not, doing just that . . .

**Later Today**

Vernon has just been informed that we're now fully operational. He charges off to tell the sergeants.

So next time the Tannoy crackles forth: 'Stand by for broadcast. All operational crews to report to the Briefing Room at 'X' hrs. I repeat. All operational crews to report to the Briefing Room at 'X' hrs. Message ends,' it means *us* also.

And I'm entering nothing more in this Diary until the Tannoy does just that. It's meant to be a Diary of 30 Operational Flights against the enemy and so far the nearest we've been to the Continent was Bognor Regis where we strayed off course slightly during a training flight . . .

**31 May 1944**

When we learned that 'G' for George was to be our Lanc for our first op, we all went out to her bay to go over her thoroughly, the fact that we'd flown in her twice before being completely beside the point – daft to take anything for granted. Vernon fiddled around in the pilot's seat and as I passed him on my way forward grinned that the only thing he was *always* worried about was the possibility that he might take off with the pitot head cover unremoved. I had a quick look at the bomb sight, then, on the right of it, at the computing mechanism: after that, a glance, on the other side, at the bomb-selector switches together with those governing the nose and tail fuse-settings; also at the bomb-distributor mechanism and its selector arm. Satisfied, I crawled further forward then straightened myself upwards into the front turret where I examined the Brownings and the loaded ammo trays. Also checked the positions of the intercom socket and the oxygen connector (two items I'd forgotten to check in my bomb-aimer's compartment). That done, I dropped down again out of the turret, crawled back through my bomb-aimer's compartment, checking the two forgotten items as I did so, to find my exit blocked by Griggs who was checking some of his instruments. Some bad language, although not ill-tempered, on my part and he squeezed aside to let me out. Vernon was still sitting in his pilot's seat, but by now was simply staring vacantly ahead. Edging past, I nodded at Norman in his navigator's compartment, but it was Dunn I wished to speak to. Told him I wanted him to come aft with me to the photo-flash housing. Knew he'd most certainly been briefed on his duty concerning the photo-flash, but there's nothing like being sure. This duty of his is to release the flash manually if it doesn't leave the Lanc when I drop the bombs. At the housing, I pointed out the release lever and told him that all he had to do was to press it downwards. 'Just like that?' he asked. *And pressed it.* The photo-flash thumped down on the tarmac with a loud thud. It did not, thank God, detonate. I think seven bods broke all existing records in getting out of that aircraft. Amid a barrage of swearing, an armourer was sent for. He said nothing but gave Dunn a dirty look. Not that any of us told him it was Dunn's fault, but we were still swearing away at him so the armourer didn't have to be very bright to know the culprit. He examined the flash, returned it to its housing, gave Dunn another dirty look and departed.

Bet Dunn will from now on be known as 'Photo-flash' in the Sergeants' Mess. For boobs like that soon get around.

So that's a check over 'G' for George completed. Will, of course, do an even more thorough check when we climb into her tonight for our first op. Don't know, of course, what the target is. All we know is that it's to be a pretty late take-off.

**31 May 1944**

That's it now; the Tannoy. First op coming up. Wonder what the target will be: maybe a nasty effort over the Reich, maybe an easier one to France. Well, will find out at Briefing.

My stomach has tightened bringing with it quite a dull ache. The explanation's perfectly simple: fear.

Also fear when I contemplate the main kite that's going to be hunting us – the ME110. (Well, if it's not exactly fear it's at least an awesome trepidation which makes your throat a bit on the dry side). The ME110 which, in the Battle of Britain was used sometimes as a fighter-bomber, sometimes as a straight fighter, but which had to be withdrawn from the Battle because of its inadequacy against the Spitfires and Hurricanes; but which had now been converted to a powerful nightfighter. It is the most heavily armed of all the Luftwaffe's defending fighters carrying two 20mm and two 30mm cannon plus another two 20mm cannon under its fuselage: some versions also carry four 210mm rockets under their wings. Let *that* creep up on your tail long enough to give you even a short burst . . . dammit, I don't even have to finish this sentence.

God, I sometimes wonder why I let myself in for all this. Nobody asked me to. I actually volunteered: and binded away at all sorts of authority to get here that much quicker. Must be round the twist. And yet, having written that, if out of the blue a sudden order came for me to go back to the safety of Canada to instruct again I'd do my nut. Actually, in this unlikely event I think for the first time since joining I'd refuse to obey a direct order given to me by the RAF (and why do some people keep on referring to the Service as 'The Raff'? It rhymes with 'riff' and is a very sloppy way of referring to the Royal Air Force).

But here's that first op coming up: wish it were over.

| | |
|---|---|
| *Op. No. 1* | *31 May – 1 June 1944* |
| *Target* | Marshalling Yards, TERGNIER |
| *A/C 'G'* | *Load* 11 x 1,000lbs.<br>2x 500lbs. |
| *Take off* | 23:39hrs. *Duration* 5.40hrs. |
| *Height* | 8,000ft. |
| *Flak* | Very light and spasmodic |
| *S/Ls* | Do. |
| *E/A* | Evasive action taken several times, but no combats |

8 A/C missing from whole night's operations which were very extensive and covered many railway centres etc. in France. None missing from Wickenby. Target well plastered as far as I could make out.

That knot was still in my stomach at Briefing, the fact that No. 1 was to be an 'easy' op like the marshalling yards at Tergnier not lessening it at all. Stayed with me even as we were driven out to the bay where 'G' for George was parked. Began to diminish as I inspected my bombs, checked my machine guns and so on. Diminished more as we climbed in and secured the hatch. Became no longer conscious of it as Vernon gave the thumbs-up sign to the two airmen operating the starter mechanism and the port-inner engine burst into life to be followed by the starboard inner then the starboard outer and, finally, the port-outer. After testing the Merlins and the magnetos, plus a crew check-round over the intercom, he eased the Lanc around until it was lined up directly with the exit from the bay. A short wait while another Lanc on the perimeter track rolled past the exit then we were out ourselves on to the track and round it. Held up at the chequered caravan while this Lanc. before us took off. As it did, Vernon edged our Lanc forward into the position thus vacated. Next we got the green Aldis and Vernon swung her round on to the runway. Another green and he lined the Lanc. up with the path of the runway. Maximum pressure on the brakes now, then, together with Griggs, he opened all four throttles wide. The engines strained for their freedom, which was given when Vernon released the brakes. The Lanc. raced forward along the runway rapidly gathering speed. We were almost running out of the concrete when Vernon eased back on the control column and lifted her very smoothly into the air.

Up came the undercart and we started climbing over base. Oxygen masks on at 5,000ft. At 8,000ft. we set course for France. I made good pin-points over England, keeping us so dead on track that we hit the French coast exactly as briefed. (Sounds self-satisfied that, but it's so terribly important to keep exactly on track – in the bomber stream, that is – if you want to avoid the risk of being picked up by a roving night-fighter.)

At the French coast some flak. Hard at first to realise it's aimed at you! But not much of it really, and none of it actually hit us. Some more flak here and there across Northern France. As I've noted above, we took evasive action once or twice, but maybe we were over-reacting. Still, better to over-react a hundred times than not to react on that fatal one time.

Then we were over Tergnier with its light and spasmodic flak. Down went the bombs, then, with bomb doors closed, we turned for base. Some more light flak, then the French coast, then the English coast, then base.

But what an easy one for our first op. A very gentle blooding, one might observe. Still, it's the first over. Only another 29 to do . . .

**Later**

Note that, this being the end of the month, my log book has been made up. Total flying hours at Wickenby to date 9.05 day and 17.10 night; including, or course, 5.40 night hours for our first op. Signed by F/L Corry who is O.C. 'A' Flight.

**2 June 1944**

Flew over RAF Lindholme earlier today on a training flight (though I think we're on ops tonight). This Yorkshire station is one of the easiest to recognise from the air: it houses No. 1656 Conversion Unit (conversion from two-engined bombers to four-engined ones – in Lindholme's case to Halifaxes – and you can soon differentiate between this airfield and the others by the wrecked Halibags lying all around it. They're all over the place. Seems converting from Wellingtons to Halibags is no piece of cake.) The converting didn't cause Vernon much difficulty, and the rest of us seemed to cope OK with the heavy, so after 21 hours day and about the same number of hours night (which took us five weeks to log) we were pronounced fit for conversion to Lancasters.

Which took us to the Lanc. School at Hemswell. Six hours converting to Lancs. and that's us ready for posting to an operational Squadron.

So that's it: been a long journey of aircrew training starting with Initial Training Wing in Scotland and ranging through Arizona and parts of Canada until you began to get in on the 'earnest' stuff back in Scotland again at a navigational and bombing school, where you flew in Ansons. After that, off to Wymeswold in Leicestershire there to convert to Wellington bombers. It's at this stage that you begin to scent that the 'pay off' is just over the horizon. And that's the possible stage we're at right now.

Maybe should record that here at Wickenby, Lincolnshire, there are two Squadrons of Lancasters – Nos. 12 and 626. No. 12 Squadron was the original unit sent to Wickenby. 'C' Flight of that Squadron was formed into 626 Squadron – hence the affinity between the two.

For a maximum effort each Squadron can put up 20-22 Lancasters (though often not as many as that). If my arithmetic is correct, such a maximum effort would entail over 207 tons of nastiness that RAF Wickenby, on one operation, can bestow upon the Third Reich and/or Occupied Europe.

Also, in all honesty, should record that the Lanc. is a kite you fall in love with – though I admit that's rather an inane sentiment to express about such a horrendous weapon of war.

Details of the Lanc: Four Rolls-Royce Merlin engines. Crew of 7. Length 68.9ft. Height 19.5ft. Wing span 102ft. Maximum loaded weight 68,000lbs. Cruising speed 216mph. Maximum speed 266mph. Ceiling 20,000ft. Bombload 14,000lbs (with fuel for 1,660 miles). Armament: twin .303 Brownings in front turret: same in mid-upper turret; four in rear turret.

| | |
|---|---|
| *Op. No. 2* | *2–3 June 1944* |
| *Target* | Radar installations at BERNAVILLE |
| *A/C 'H'* | *Load* 1x4,000lbs.<br>16x 500lbs. |
| *Take off* | 23:40 hrs. *Duration* 4.20 hrs. |
| *Height* | 8,000ft. |
| *Flak* | Light, but some bursts quite close to a/c – especially over target |
| *S/Ls* | Practically nil |
| *E/A* | No sightings |

Nineteen a/c missing from the whole night's ops which included railway marshalling yards at Frappes and many other small sorties. None missing from Wickenby.

Again had that knot in my stomach at Briefing. Not such a tight one, though, signifying perhaps a miniscule reduction in my fear factor. Did flinch a bit, however, when, over the target, the flak started bursting all around us. (Get the impression that the Germans are firing at us and us alone). But this was another easy effort. Would be inclined to say it was a piece of cake were it not for the thought that sooner or later we have to do the long, dangerous haul to the Reich – maybe even to the Big City (which is what Berlin is called). Reckon it will be later rather than sooner, though – the Invasion has to come first. And that can't be so very far away now, what with all this business of bombing rail junctions, marshalling yards, radar installations and such-like. Rumour hath it that 'Butch' (that's Air Marshall Sir Arthur Harris to everybody except the air crews in Bomber Command) isn't at all happy at his 'heavies' being diverted from their task of laying waste the Third Reich to engage in this kind of work. As for me, and the crew, we're all for it – the more of those 'easy efforts' the happier we'll all be . . .

**3 June 1944**

Glad – no, that's not the word; even 'grateful' wouldn't do justice – that we came here to Wickenby in early May rather than mid-March. For that earlier arrival here assuredly would have seen us on the Nuremburg raid of 30/31 March when 12 Squadron put up thirteen Lancs. and 626 Squadron fifteen, out of a total force of 795 bombers. Evidently things went wrong from the start and the bomber stream began to straggle at a comparatively early stage thus spreading themselves out and making easier targets for the night-fighters which were vectored on to them from all parts of the Reich.

Also, being scattered, the bombers presented ideal targets for the numerous flak batteries not only over Nuremburg but along the route. The Luftwaffe had a field day. Of the 795 bombers attacking Nuremburg, 94 failed to return: also of the 17 supplying the French Resistance, one was lost; and a further 12 crashed on return to England. Some losses, 107 heavies. There would also have been, of course, a larger number which made it back to base but which were seriously damaged and probably out of action for some considerable time. But 107: that's 749 bods. Yes, to have arrived here in the middle of March rather than early May would have seen us on that Nuremburg disaster. Of that I am certain. Equally certain that, being a raw and inexperienced aircrew, we would have bought it. Odd the part luck plays in it all; when training on Ansons at Wigtown I developed appendicitis; the decision was that I must have my appendix removed before going on ops, the Medical Officer explaining that if I were shot down the required medical facilities might not be available; and so my entry to the operational field was delayed by a couple of months. Long enough for me to miss some of those earlier affairs over Berlin and other German cities with their horrendous losses. Also long enough for me to miss becoming a statistic over Nuremburg.

Luck: nothing else.

| | |
|---|---|
| *Op No 3* | *4–5 June 1944* |
| *Target* | Heavy railway gun installations at SANGATTE (PAS DE CALAIS) |
| *A/C 'H'* | *Load* 18 x 500lbs. |
| *Take off* | 01:55 hrs. *Duration* 3.15 hrs. |
| *Height* | 7,000ft. |
| *Flak* | Practically nil |
| *S/Ls* | Nil (10/10ths cloud over target) |
| *E/A* | Two night fighters sighted. Near enough to us to identify them – a JU88 and an ME109. They were moving from starboard to port across our tail, but (obviously) did not sight us. However, we took violent evasive action. The mid-upper fired a short burst at them. To me, that was daft; it gave our position away<br>No aircraft missing from the entire night's operations which were mainly on targets along the northern French coast |

Yes, it's definitely pre-invasion stuff: your head doesn't have to come to a point to be able to work that out; those heavy railway guns were obviously centred on the Channel. But, on the other hand, why so little Luftwaffe activity? The Germans, what with all this bombing of railway junctions, heavy gun installations and so on, must have worked out that the Invasion isn't very far away. So why not move the night-fighters from the Reich – which seems to be getting off rather more lightly these days – to France? Very puzzling.

No tightening of the stomach muscles on this occasion; not even a faint quiver. Tell myself not to feel just so cocky, that when we get briefed for an op on Germany those wretched muscles will start working overtime.

| | |
|---|---|
| *Op. No. 4* | *5–6 June 1944* |
| *Target* | Heavy gun battery at CRISBECQ |
| *A/C 'H'* | *Load* 11 x 1,000lbs.<br>4 x 500lbs. |
| *Take off* | 21:10 hrs. *Duration* 4.35 hrs. |
| *Height* | 7,000ft. |
| *Flak* | Practically nil |
| *S/Ls* | Nil |
| *E/A* | JU 88 sighted and evasive action taken: he did not attack |

This is it: the Invasion of Europe. This is what all that goods yards and railway junction bashing has been about. As we enter the Briefing Room each of us gets a letter from Ike. (But, surprisingly enough, most of us just seem to glance at it rather superficially.) At the Briefing they're much more intense than usual: they tell us that this heavy gun battery at Crisbecq has simply *got* to be put out of action, no matter the cost: if it is not eliminated, the Invasion might well be affected to a frightening degree. They made it sound so emotional that any minute I expected the Heavenly violins to start whispering.

But talk about Secrets! Seems as if everybody, but everybody, at Wickenby is out there at the runway to wave us off. And they look as if they're cheering but, of course, obviously we can't hear them.

But not only air force types. There are one or two farms just off the aircraft bays and I see farm workers and their wives and children gathered together waving madly to us.

Yes, some Secret! But I don't suppose it matters now – obviously the Invasion fleet has left its various ports, of which the Germans must be aware; and is heading for its destination, of which the Germans also must be aware.

We attacked the battery at 23:25hrs. I made a good run-up to it and am pretty certain I obtained some direct hits. (Later it was reported as having been obliterated: if so, it certainly gave the Invasion fleet no trouble).

As we returned to base across the Channel, we saw masses of aircraft heading towards France. So many different types, it would take about five lines to record them.

But the Luftwaffe: just that JU88 which I sighted, nothing else. Surely with this being the Invasion they'd shove up every available aircraft. But, so far, no.

The Invasion itself took place in the early hours of the morning.

Bet we're turned round after a short break during which they can refuel and re-arm the Lancs and are then put on to bombing railway junctions slightly inland from the French coast.

**6 June 1944**

An order via the Tannoy for this afternoon: for an aircraft and ship recognition exercise in the Briefing Room. No roll-call or anything like that – if you don't turn up it could be your own funeral. It was conducted by a F/O navigator from 626 Squadron who seems to specialise in the subject. Good, too. By our book we could recognise at a glance every aircraft currently flown by the Luftwaffe: but not by this chap's book. A quick, split-second flash of a part of an aircraft and 'what's that?' 'No, it isn't a ME109; it's a Spitfire.' And so on. Then: 'Now, bet none of you bods know what *this* is.' We didn't. 'A Morane fighter. When the French collapsed in 1940 the Germans came across crates and crates of them stacked at manufacturers, stacked at French airfields, in fact stacked all over the place. And the Luftwaffe uses them quite often on various duties. So now you know what to do if you come across one.'

This F/O then went on to show slides of some Eye-tye aircraft. When a shot of a Fiat CR42, which is a bi-plane fighter, came on to the screen, I informed the gathering that I'd seen one shot down over England during the Battle of Britain. To which Horsfall replied that I must have confused it with a Gloster Gladiator. But I hadn't. Windbag Musso had begged Hitler to permit his heroic flyers to share in the destruction of the Royal Air Force and had, grudgingly, been permitted to use a number of airfields in Northern France. His force of Caproni bombers, escorted by Fiat CR42 fighters, had taken off to bomb RAF airfields. At first sight of the Spits the Capronis had turned and fled, accompanied by nearly all their escort. This one had continued on. And when I saw him he was being attacked by a frustrated Spitfire, doing very steep turns whenever the Spit dived. Eventually the Fiat landed somewhere nearby and that was the last I saw of him.

When others joined Horsfall in questioning all this, the aircraft-identification F/O came to my assistance by confirming what I had said: also by showing a slide of a Caproni bomber. At which I saluted Horsfall with two fingers and reminded myself to buy the F/O a pint sometime.

Next we moved on to Jap aircraft with a slide of the Zero which, we were informed, was one of the best fighters so far produced in WW II. Then one of a Mitsubishi bomber which he didn't seem to think much of. But, most of us, having no intention whatsoever of doing any flying in the Far East, paid scant attention. This was the stage when our instructor produced what he referred to as his 'awakeners' which were nudes (usually from *Men Only*). These were watched with rather more interest, but our navigator, Sgt. Norman, who was sitting next to me, intimated in a loud voice, that, to him, they were pretty tame stuff and hadn't he (the F/O) anything a bit more exciting? This request received almost unanimous vocal support plus a stamping of feet. 'I have,' came the retort, 'but you're not going to see it until we've done Ship Recognition.'

Groans all round. Most, like me, couldn't tell the difference between a pocket battleship and a destroyer. And, in any case, nobody in their right mind ever flies near, far less across, a line of ships, because, even if they *were* RN, they fire on you nevertheless. Honestly, I don't think they teach Aircraft Recognition in our Navy, their attitude seeming to be that if it's in the air it shouldn't be so fire at it.

Once the groans had died down the F/O flashed on the screen for the briefest of seconds a shot of an orgy in full flight.

'*That's* more like it,' announced Sgt. Norman. 'And it's all you're going to see until we've done a spot of Ship Recognition,' intimated our instructor. A clever one that – knew his air-crew. Should have been promoted F/L ages ago.

So we suffered the ship stuff. And, after it, the F/O intimated: 'All right, you crowd of sex-starved maniacs, here it is.' And on came the orgy scene.

'Got it the wrong way up,' said someone.

'No it isn't: You have to turn your head sideways,' explained another.

'Godammit, that's one for the books,' breathed Vernon whom, I had felt up until then, didn't go much for that sort of thing.

A couple of seconds later. 'OK, that's it,' from the F/O as he switched off.

'Any more and you'll all go out of here and start raping the WAAFs.' '*They'll* be lucky,' grimaced some sergeant as we started rising from our seats.

Which remark brought the proceedings to an end.

When I returned to my billet I found that Cliff – our shared batman – had left a football coupon on my bed. (He'll have become a collector, I suppose; never misses the chance to make an odd bob.) Hadn't realised that the Pools were no longer individual like Littlewoods, Vernons and so on; they are called Unity Pools and have the names of all the bigger Pools Promoters on them. The coupon is for this coming Saturday (10 June) and all the teams are Scottish. Know so little about the game that I wasn't aware that the football seasons differed between England and Scotland. Decide to fill it up and start off with forecasting Hibs to draw with Airdrie both at half and full-time. That done, I suddenly tear the bloody thing to pieces. Sounds superstitious – and a bit silly – but have the feeling that if I were to win a most welcome packet on the Pools I'd get a rather different and most *un*welcome packet from another source.

**Later**

. . . Harking back to the Zero mentioned above, an Aussie sergeant-pilot told me later that the Australians, to counter the bombing of Darwin by the Japs, set up the latest in radar stations, equipped the RAAF with a squadron of the latest Spits piloted mostly by Aussie bods who'd fought in the Battle of Britain and then sat back with joyful anticipation to await the next Japanese air raid on Darwin. When it came the escorting Zeros, to the horror of the RAAF, shot down a goodly number of the Spits. An American pilot, who'd flown with Chenault in China, explained to the RAAF that their tactics were all wrong, that the heavier Spit could not cope in a dog-fight with the nimble Zero. The only possible tactics were for the Spits to await the raiders at height – which they were able to do thanks to the radar units – then to dive down through the Jap formation cannon and machine guns ablaze: to then use the speed they'd built up in the dive to regain height and do the same again. This the Spits did. And created such havoc among the Japs that they have never raided Darwin again.

Could be true, I suppose, with the Spit being armoured and also carrying the weight of sophisticated gadgetry and the Zero being unarmoured, basically just a simple, unsophisticated kite. First time I'd heard it, though.

| | |
|---|---|
| *Op. No. 5* | *5 – 7 June 1944* |
| *Target* | Railway junction at ACHERES (PARIS) |
| *A/C 'H'* | *Load* 18 x 500lbs. |
| *Take off* | 23:45 hrs. *Duration* 5.10 hrs. |
| *Height* | 7,000ft. |
| *Flak* | Nil |
| *S/Ls* | Nil |
| *E/A* | Nil |

Duff weather – heavy cloud and rain. Was map-reading my way quite easily up to the target – had even selected and fused my bombs – when the Master Bomber of the Pathfinders Force came on the air and ordered us to take our bombs back to base. Having real finger trouble the PFF, not being able to identify the railway junction. (Yet, to be fair, perhaps the cloud beneath the Master Bomber was much thicker than the stuff below us.) Was annoying, really, to be able to identify that rail junction so clearly, even to see it sliding so steadily up my bombsight towards the graticule (as you get it on to the graticule you press the tit) then to be told not to bomb it. Felt inclined to press the tit despite the order, but thought better of it. Not that I'm becoming 'bomb-happy' or anything like that, but for all I know, because we didn't bomb, a German troop train – maybe even carrying Tiger tanks which can knock hell, so we understand, out of any tanks we or the Yanks possess – bound for Normandy might as a result be able to pass through that junction before dawn.

So we returned to base with our bomb load. Our turn over Acheres brought us over the outskirts of Paris. They don't have a black-out there; it's a form of 'blue-out' and you can see, dimly, the outlines of certain streets. Now and then torches could be seen flashing 'V'. Suppose the French would have to stand on roofs to do that, otherwise the Germans would shoot them.

No flak or searchlights over Paris. In fact, this evening we haven't had flak or searchlights anywhere.

Wonder if I'll ever visit Paris. Before the war only the comparatively rich could afford to visit France (when everything was very cheap a bottle of wine, I'm told, costing about a tanner). Maybe my turn will come after the war.

Seven aircraft missing from this operation – though none from Wickenby – which shows that there must have been quite a few night fighters knocking around. Surprising they made so many kills what with all that heavy cloud and without searchlights to guide them: reckon their victims must have been Lancs who got out of the bomber stream and were then sitting ducks, easily picked up by the radar sets the night-fighters are supposed to be able to use with great accuracy once the German ground control has guided them to the vicinity of the wandering Lanc. It's the old, old story; allow yourselves to get out of the bomber stream and almost certainly you have had it. Even on a five hour round trip into Northern France.

**7 June 1944**

Told today (though I haven't seen it in writing) that in the event of an abort before we take off we are to hand back our Iron Rations. These are usually a tin of orange juice, chocolate, chewing gum and glucose sweets: and always a Mars bar. And they want them back if you don't actually go: what some people will do for the sake of saving 3d on a Mars bar! But this presents no problem at all to us: we eat our rations before we even get *into* the Lanc: we always did: sometimes it makes us feel slightly sick.

The Escape Kit's a different matter and you have to sign for it. That's because of the money it contains: French francs, Belgian francs, German marks, Spanish pesetas, etc. Quite a lot of ackers, which they don't mind your using if shot down, but also which they don't want you to consider your own here in the UK. (On the subject of pesetas, the Intelligence types say that if you make Spain and run out of them you can promise a genuine helper who actually gets you to the British Legation a 'reasonable' sum of money and that this promise will be honoured. They do not specify what 'reasonable' amounts to). The kit is enclosed in a sort of mica, but is supposed to be quite easy to open. It also contains pills for making water safe, some toilet paper, other pills to give you energy. And I think that's all. Except for a pack of three fags and a small book of matches. The fags won't be of Virginian tobacco, that's for sure. They'll probably be of Algerian tobacco. This because Virginian is unobtainable in Germany and Occupied Europe (at least for civilians) and walking along a street puffing away at a fag containing Virginian could attract official attention your way, which would lead to your complete undoing.

On the subject of undoing, Vernon has been told to watch his eating habits if he's shot down and manages to evade. Not a criticism of Vernon's actual table manners, but a warning to avoid conveying food to his mouth as he does in the Mess. Like nearly all Americans, he uses knife and fork to cut his food into mouth-size portions after which he transfers fork to his right hand and then uses it on its own. All Gestapo on the lookout for evaders have been briefed on this American eating habit and to eat this way in a restaurant is almost tantamount to be sitting there wearing Allied uniform. We have been told that quite a few Yanks, bailing out of their Fortresses and being picked up by the Resistance, have given themselves away by eating thus.

But other things can give you away too and you don't have to be a Yank. Things you simply don't think of. One of our chaps thought he had it all going for him: there he was in Lyons, walking well behind his contact who was guiding him to the railway station. All was well: next the train, then some mountaineering, then Spain, then back to England. He felt happy; he started whistling. He was still whistling at the railway station. The Gestapo picked him up immediately. No wonder: listening to foreign broadcasts is a punishable offence. So how came he to be whistling: 'We'll Meet Again'? Easily done, though.

**7 June 1944**

Nothing on this evening, so I cycled into Lincoln. That's a wonderful bike I have. A Raleigh my step-father bought me in 1936. Cost four guineas plus an extra guinea for a Sturmey-Archer 3 speed gear. I started carting it around with me when I returned from Canada. It's a tough, sturdy bit of work which so far has survived the hazards of travelling in guards' vans on the LNER, LMS and GW railways, of lying around somewhere in Ansons when, with a few days' leave to my credit, I sometimes obtained a lift (under the guise of a training flight) to a not-so-distant airfield, spent a day or so in an adjoining town, then cycled back to wherever I was based; also of being borrowed constantly at Wickenby by all sorts of unauthorised persons. But to date it hasn't been whipped, for which I must be thankful.

Once in Lincoln I cycled about for a while, taking in the sights. Then I spotted, towards evening, a notice intimating that a swing pianist named George Shearing was giving a performance at 7 pm in the Corn Exchange. I'm very fond of swing music so decided to look in on it. That guy's blind (I found out), but he's got a sound there that is simply out of this world. Was absolutely enthralled by his performance. I'm no musician, but his phrasing, his rhythm – oh, just his everything – could keep you there all night listening to him. Which I nearly did; three encores and still cries for more. We'll certainly hear more of George Shearing, of that I am sure.

As I cycled back to Wickenby (very pleasant I found it, cycling in the dark and hearing all the animal noises coming from the vegetation at the side of the road – surprisingly loud, because they don't hear the approach of a bicycle), I found myself reflecting that it was high time we had here in Britain an outfit which could produce a 'new' sound like Shearing's. Until the war, we had 'dance bands' like Henry Hall (God, if I ever hear 'Teddy Bears Picnic' even *once* more, I think I'll throw in the towel!), Jack Hylton, Billy Cotton and so on. Must admit that Ambrose had a pretty good band, though.

But he never played really good swing: the only good swing music played in Britain was by a West Indian – Ken 'Snake-hips' Johnston – but he was killed when a bomb fell on the Café de Paris in London in 1942.

But the RAF has come to the rescue! It has two outfits which are quite excellent. One of them is the Squadronaires which I believe started out as the RAF Dance Orchestra, and the other is the Skyrockets which started out as the No. 1 Balloon Centre Dance Orchestra. Make most of the pre-war outfits sound pretty mediocre and third rate.

When I arrived back at Wickenby, I found I was without my Form 1250 (my RAF Identity card). Being the proud owner of *two* Number One Uniforms, I usually knock around Wickenby in my older, and scruffier, effort and retain my newer one for going out. I keep my 1250 in my left-hand breast pocket. I had forgotten to transfer it from the scruffy to the smart. Naturally, the guard at the gate wouldn't let me in and I was escorted to the Guard Room to await the Duty Officer. The DO, who had gone to bed, though strictly speaking I suppose he should not have, was summoned. He was a non-flying type. He was not at all happy, the time now being 02:00 hrs. And he was *not* the least bit interested in George Shearing, especially at being acquainted with this pianist's performance in the middle of his lecture on the iniquities of going around without one's Form 1250. But I was admitted. The DO, having now calmed down somewhat, invited me to his office for a cup of tea. But he was still not interested in George Shearing.

**8 June 1944**

By order – no exceptions. The entire Station strength on parade. To witness what to me anyway was a sad, sad sight. We were well away from the 'action' so I couldn't hear exactly all of what was being said. But I certainly could see what was being *done.* This sergeant had refused to fly on an op. He had been accused, and found guilty, of LMF, which is Lack of Moral Fibre. There he was standing out there in front, all on his own, in full view of every person on the unit, to be stripped of his wings (or his half wing – I couldn't see) followed by his sergeant's tapes. Reduced from sergeant to AC2 in the space of a minute (they would all be unstitched beforehand, of course). All this followed by an immediate posting elsewhere.

Vernon says he feels sorry for the guy. Horsefall says it serves him bloody well right, that the RAF had spent a packet on training him and that the time to chicken out was *before* you find yourself in the kitchen. Maybe they're both right: if the chap had done, say 15 or 20 ops and his nerve had failed him, well, it was a raw deal he'd got. But if it was after only his second or third op, well, what else could he have expected? (Wonder what the Germans would have done in these circumstances?)

I make no attempt to find out this sergeant's name. I'm glad I was too far back to hear it.

Incidentally, difference between an NCO and Officer who is LMF is that the latter is cashiered. He becomes a civilian – for about two days. Then he is called up – some say by the Army as the RAF don't want him again, even as an airman.

| | |
|---|---|
| *Op. No. 6* | *9 June 1944* |
| *Target* | Fighter aerodrome at FLERS |
| *A/C 'J'* | *Load* 18 x 500lbs. |
| *Take off* | 00:38 hrs. *Duration* 5.10 hrs. |
| *Height* | 4,000ft. |
| *Flak* | Nil |
| *S/Ls* | Nil |
| *E/A* | Nil |

Pretty cloudy. Saw what I think were my bombs straddle the Target Indicators. Target seemed to be well pranged.

And this counts as an op! The tour is 30 no matter whether all are on soft, easy targets such as this or whether all are on the Ruhr. Just luck, I suppose, whether you get the easy ones or the really dicey efforts. Well, it can't last – this easy stuff, I mean. Sooner or later Bomber Command will be released from backing up the Invasion forces and will return to its original task of laying the Third Reich flat. Which is what they bloody well deserve. Bet the Germans aren't as much for Hitler as they were when he had Europe at their feet.

One spot of carelessness on this effort, though, which could have cost us our lives. My carelessness at that; nobody else's. The drill is that, once the bombs have been dropped, I tell Vernon and ask him to close the bomb lay doors: after he has done this, and announced it, I take the Aldis and shine it up the bay to check that what I have said indeed is true – that none of our bombs is still with us. I forgot to do my check until we were about 10 to 15 minutes on our way back from Flers. And when I slid back the panel and shone the lamp into the bay there they were: three 500 pounders, all fused, rolling about on the floor of the bay. I screamed at Vernon to open the bomb bay doors, adding why. This he did. And the three bombs dropped through the night on to somewhere in France. I hoped it was some French field which received them – not some innocent French village. But that I shall never know: it's something I refuse to think about.

'What the f . . . happened there?' asked Vernon once the bomb bay doors were closed again.

I couldn't answer: probably, when I'd pressed the tit, these three bombs had come slightly adrift from their cradles, but not sufficiently enough to free them: then the movement of the Lanc had gradually eased them away from the cradles and on to the bomb bay floor. Where, all fused, they rolled around merely waiting for something to detonate them: such as a violent corkscrewing to evade a night fighter.

We didn't, of course, mention at de-briefing. But I had a word on the side with the chieffy armourer who promised to check the release mechanism on all our cradles.

**9 June 1944**

Mess Meeting announced for this afternoon. You can't get out of it; no officer permitted to be absent unless on some absolutely essential duty. Vernon, Horsefall and myself secure seats right at the back of the ante-room, out of the Mess President's immediate eye as we feel happier there than sitting directly in front of him. The routine business over, the President arrives at 'Any Other Business'. At which stage someone nearer the front (I'm almost certain it's Sandy Mansfield, the S/L Bombing Leader of No. 12) accuses the Mess of sharp practice over messing. In a voice from which all warmth has departed, the President asks him to explain himself. Sandy says, well, we get eggs and bacon on return from an op, don't we? The President intones that this is a fact he and anybody who isn't a congenital idiot is perfectly well aware of. Then Sandy goes on to say in that beautifully languid voice of his, yes, but only slightly under half of us so often don't return so what happens to the *rest* of the eggs and bacon? Does the Mess do a crafty piece of flogging, for instance? The silence which follows isn't just pregnant – it's eight months gone. The President ends this silence by saying that such an accusation is most unwarranted and ungentlemanly and suggests that it should be withdrawn immediately and unreservedly. Sandy apologises, withdraws it completely, but says he just wondered where the unconsumed woof went, that's all.

Actually, as a result of this,from then on we get our eggs and bacon *before* we go on an op. Rumour hath it that the Mess President, in authorising this, said that 'well, any of these bastards being shot down will at least do so with full bellies'. I'm told, incidentally, that he is on his second tour and that he's got over 40 ops under his belt. (In the event, we now also get eggs and bacon when we get back. If we do).

On the subject of eggs and bacon, these fresh eggs, which are in very short supply all over the country, are for operational air crew only. A bit embarrassing at times for you to sit down and be served with a delightful fresh, fried egg while beside you some ground-crew officer is trying to force down that dreadful powdered egg which I for my part find absolutely inedible. Wouldn't give it to the cat. The cat wouldn't eat it anyway.

| | |
|---|---|
| *Op. No. 7* | *11–12 June 1944* |
| *Target* | Railroad marshalling yards at EVREUX |
| *A/C 'K'* | *Load* 11 x 1,000lbs.<br>4 x 500lbs. |
| *Take off* | 22:15 hrs. *Duration* 4:40 hrs. |
| *Height* | 2,500ft. |
| *Flak* | Very occasional indeed along the route – hardly enough to comment on – but over target the light flak (from 88s, I should think) was very accurate, bursting all around the a/c, virtually cocooning it. Heard it rattling around on the outside of the fuselage |
| *S/Ls* | Nil |
| *E/A* | Nil (but on return some crews reported sightings) |

Nine-tenths cloud over target, but was able – flying as low as 2,500ft. – to spot the marshalling yards surprisingly clearly. There seemed to be quite a few trains in the yards; you'd think they'd be able to damp down the engines when informed of the likelihood of an air attack – I could see the steam rising quite clearly from at least a couple of locomotives. Would be troop or ammo trains, of course: doubt if any civilian traffic would be permitted in these parts. I am so fond of railways and engines that I get no satisfaction from bombing such installations. Yet it's got to be done accurately: absolutely no point in taking off with a bomb load of 13,000lbs, exposing yourself to danger getting here (and getting back again) and then, when over the target, being slip-shod and careless. I have a good run-in, get a good aiming point and drop them in series right across the marshalling yards. Some mighty explosions which suggest ammo train coming skywards.

But some bomb aimer has been careless (maybe more than one bomb aimer) because, before we left, we saw fires raging in the SE part of the adjoining town. It's this 'drop-back' that they keep on and on about at briefing: bomb aimers lying there, thumb poised over the tit all ready to press and the target sliding slowly – oh, so slowly – up the graticule: and they can't wait – their thumb drops just that fraction of a second before the target is fully on the cross graticle and, gradually, if one or two bomb-aimers act similarly, the entire bombing effort more or less creeps backwards, until it's the area *before* the target which is getting it, not the target itself. They're quite extensive fires and I wonder how many French people die as a result. Also how many French railway workers are killed in our attack on the yards.

The French – difficult to assess one's feelings for them. True, they packed in without a fight, but then the 1914–1918 War, where so many Frenchmen died in the trenches, probably had much to do with this. And yet, the Germans suffered massive casualties in that War too, which doesn't seem to have detracted from their fighting capabilities. Maybe if the French had had a Hitler . . .

| | |
|---|---|
| *Op. No. 8* | *12–13 June 1944* |
| *Target* | Synthetic oil refinery GELSENKIRCHEN (RUHR) |
| *A/C 'K'* | *Load* 1x4,000lbs.<br>18x500lbs. |
| *Take off* | 23:00 hrs. *Duration* 5:05 hrs. |
| *Height* | 19,000ft. |
| *Flak* | Very heavy and concentrated over target – extensive barrage. Light to medium before and after target |
| *S/Ls* | Very concentrated – three main cones . . . about 60 over target itself; 30 to the north and 40 to the south. Saw two aircraft coned |
| *E/A* | No sightings: many fighter flares dropped |

Concentrated bombing of target: heavy and widespread fires raging. Flak, S/Ls and fighter flares lit up the sky to such an extent that you could almost have read a newspaper in the a/c. See one shot down over the coast. Flak bursting all around the a/c. Rear gunner says he saw one of ours go down in flames just after target.

17 a/c missing from this raid (one from this station – P/O Williams and crew).

Luftwaffe dropped many dummy Target Indicators.

275 of our a/c took part.

First one on the Reich itself. And so bloody different: it made one feel we'd simply been playing at the game up until now. Indeed, compared to this, all those previous efforts over Occupied Europe seemed like pleasant little picnics, events you looked back upon with something akin to pleasure (if you can equate dropping bombs with that word).

Was, as per usual, in the front turret: I always climb into it shortly after we're airborne. And there was no need to be dramatic and shout: 'Enemy coast ahead.' Because all could see it, except, of course, the wireless operator and the navigator, both of whom were in their little, blacked-out compartments. Yes, you could see it: maybe not the actual coast, but the flak – seemingly solid walls of it – hosing up into the sky. We were in the second wave, so it was the first one which was getting it: that's where I saw a Lanc buying it – he just seemed to explode in mid air.

Crossing the coast, the flak (which, I'd think, was from those extra-heavy 10.5 and 12.8cm guns we'd heard about: which could have fitted – the more bombers shot down over the coast the less left to bomb the target) seemed to reach out for you alone. As if it was something personal. The searchlights too: again one received the feeling that it was *your* Lanc only that they were trying to fasten onto.

Over the coast and inland, leaving that wall of flak behind us now occupied with the third wave of Lancs. Still some flak and searchlights, of course: all predicted stuff.

But now the flares were bursting all around us, dropped, I should imagine, by Junkers 88s. Trying to illuminate us so that the night fighters could come in. They were all around and now and then I saw flurries of tracer as interceptions were made. And occasionally I saw the silhouette of other Lancs: comforting, because it confirmed that we were still in the bomber stream. Get out of the stream and you've absolutely had it: you're a sitting duck and can be picked off easily.

Next Cartwright was yelling: 'Corkscrew, corkscrew' like a man demented and Vernon had her in a stomach-wretching dive to port followed by a steep climb to starboard then another almost vertical dive, but to starboard this time. Cartwright then announced that he was certain we'd lost whatever was after us and we levelled off. Was glad to note the odd Lanc around us and that therefore we were still in the stream.

Approaching Gelsenkirchen at last. More flak than ever, it seemed: and more searchlights than ever. Fires caused by first wave intensive. Green Target Indicators for us, the second wave. I got them clearly into my sight and then down went the 4,000 pounder and the eighteen 500 pounders.

Shouted for bomb doors to be closed: flew on to turning point. As we banked for our next course I could not help staring at the fires burning below which, even from 19,000 feet, one could see clearly. Stupid doing that, really: it must have destroyed my night vision. (Was about here that rear-gunner announced he could see a Lanc. bursting into flame as it plunged earthwards).

That was really widespread bombing. What is now referred to as an 'area bash'. Some of my load must have fallen on houses; maybe even on air raid shelters as well. A faint niggling at the back of my mind; how many women and children had I killed simply by pressing that little tit? No point in deluding oneself over that – one had killed people. But I supposes it's daft to permit your mind to think along these lines. Trouble is I'm too tired. It's now almost 08:00 and, honestly, I don't know why I stay up writing this when I could be in bed and sleeping. Or trying to sleep, anyway.

One more thing before I get off. Didn't feel scared during this. Not during it: but after it felt something akin to a tremble coming on.

And yet, surely that was easy stuff compared to what the bomber crews suffered in 1942. Even last year was worse when you look back on Bomber Command's losses over it, both in air crews and aircraft. Should consider ourselves lucky, I suppose.

**13 June 1944**
We had always been well briefed for those little French affairs; by the nature of things there wasn't much to brief us on, actually.

But the Gelsenkirchen briefing was a long one dwelling, in detailed fashion, on every facet of the operation. Am therefore taking this opportunity (the Tannoy not having announced anything yet for today) of noting down some, but not all, of what went on.

I had not noticed on previous briefings the posting of an armed guard. But there was certainly one this time: at the briefing room door. As far as I could make out, once the briefing had started nobody got in, or out.

We sat together as a crew: there would be two crews in each row. Winco Nelson started calling the roll, asking the pilots to answer for their crews. All replied OK except one who said his bomb aimer had gone sick. The Winco was rather annoyed at this and asked why he hadn't been informed earlier. The pilot replied that all this had happened only five minutes ago. Sandy Mansfield, our Bombing Leader, looked quite delighted – here was his chance (he was on his second tour) to get in another. But no joy for Sandy: a bomb aimer who had just one to do to complete his tour was hanging around waiting for an opportunity such as this and he took the sick one's place.

Then Winco Nelson nodded in the direction of the sheet covering the Order of Battle board: it was removed to show the target: "Gelsenkirchen".

Some groaning at this: by those who didn't know it before from the earlier navigators' and bomb aimers' pre-briefing, which produced a smile from the Winco plus the observation that some of those present had been as far as the Ruhr before. After which he indicated the Intelligence Officer, at the same time asking for a bit more quiet.

The IO rose and, with a long pointer, indicated Gelsenkirchen provoking, from someone in the front, the observation that we all knew perfectly bloody well where it was. This he ignored and proceeded to tell us the importance to the German war effort of the various heavy industries located there, especially the synthetic oil factory, which was our main target: he quoted facts and figures which nobody really listened to. Then transferred the pointer to the Navigation Officer: at which the joker in the front congratulated them both on managing to effect this without dropping the thing.

The NO indicated the red-taped lines leading from Wickenby via the various turning etc. points to Gelsenkirchen then continuing slightly beyond the target before doubling back to base. All this, of course, was well known to the navigators through their pre-briefing and his request for questions was not, as a result, taken up.

Next it was Sandy Mansfield's turn, as Bombing Leader. Again, we as bomb aimers had had our pre-briefing and already knew the layout of the bomb load, distribution readings and so on. He therefore confined himself to stating time on target, the fact that the Target Indicators would be four reds surrounded by greens and to remember to bomb the centre of the reds. He repeated the old plea to have the reds dead on the cross of the bomb-sight and not to press the tit that fraction of a second too early and thus start the raid slipping back. He added that if we had to jettison the bomb load we'd have to do four hours' flying before landing. He concluded with his usual old hoary effort about not forgetting to fuse our bombs before dropping them. No laugh at this: neither did he expect it.

The Meteorology Officer then told us how much cloud he predicted along the route and over the target. I forget exactly how much: all I remember is that he received a subdued cheer when he predicted no cloud over Wickenby on our return.

The Gunnery Officer started off by saying: 'Right, gentlemen', which provoked an outburst of coughing. He then indicated on the map the various night fighter stations along the route making the obvious point that we could expect heavy attacks in the vicinity of them. And he repeated twice that the best method of defence was violent corkscrewing whenever anything at all was thought to be coming up behind us.

Last came the Engineering Officer's piece. It was all so very technical, about revs, boost, etc. that it conveyed nothing to me.

To wind up, Winco Nelson resumed his stance: he intimated that we'd now heard all the Leaders and went on to say that engines were to be started in various sequences. 'A' Flight first, then 'B' Flight twenty minutes later. Times of take-off for 'A' and 'B' immediately after. The signal for operation cancelled would be two red Verey lights. He ignored completely a plea from somewhere near the back praying for two reds, told us to obey the caravan and pointed out that we were to use runway number three. We were to climb to 19,000ft over Wickenby (done by a completely monotonous to-and-froing) and to time ourselves by reaching that height by (I forget the time: think it was about midnight). We were to maintain 19,000 all the way to the target, but to drop to 15,000ft by the time we'd reached the first turning point beyond it. After hitting the English coast, we were to drop height enough to arrive back over Wickenby at 6,000ft. He then pointed at a heavy white line across northern France and said that this represented the limit of the advance of our Armies to date: under no circumstances whatsoever were we to jettison bombs between this line and the coast: neither were we to jettison within 30 miles inland of the line (presumably to take into account possible advances of our own forces).

Winco Nelson concluded by yet again warning about the

bombing slipping back along our approach route. One kite, he said, does it, then another, and, before you know it, the entire effort of the operation is nullified; the suburbs of the target area have been pranged and the principal object of the raid has escaped virtually scot-free. I must admit that, once or twice, I've been sorely tempted to press that button just that split second too soon: and when that happens I tell myself to count to three. Which I do, as slowly as I can manage. By the 'three' the target is exactly on the cross and my sighting is bang-on. I think it is better to be a half second *late* in pressing the tit than being that half second early: if you over-shoot slightly others, sighting perhaps on the fires you raise, will plank their loads reasonably accurately.

We thought that was Winco Nelson finished. But he spent another minute or so to tell us that no Master of Ceremonies would be attending the proceedings and that if we heard anyone claiming to be such we were to ignore him – he'd be the Hun trying to play a trick on us.

He asked for questions. There was none. Before declaring the briefing over Winco Nelson reminded us that the Pathfinders would keep re-inforcing the target markers as and when necessary and that, if we saw fresh lots of reds and greens going down, we were to transfer our aiming points to them. He next gave us a sort of casual wave with his hand and wished us all the best of luck. He didn't say he wished he could come with us: he didn't have to.

Yes, a detailed, intensive briefing for Gelsenkirchen. Left us all somewhat subdued – especially those crews who, like ours, had only the French jobs behind them. Vernon it was who put it in a nutshell. 'No more farting about over France this time,' he murmured. 'We're in the big boys' league now.'

**13 June 1944**

What, yet another Mess bill! They seem to be presented with increasing frequency. But I suppose that the Mess Secretary is quite right to ensure the quick and prompt settling of Mess accounts as so many of what he refers to as his 'customers' are unlikely to be around to fork up if he doesn't get these bits of paper into our mail boxes quite smartly: I know of one or two characters who ignore their Mess bills for as long as they can just for that very reason; I don't see what satisfaction could be obtained on reflection, if shot down, that at least they didn't get their Mess bill out of you (which they do in any case – from the pay still due to you).

But each bill invariably seems to be higher than the previous one. The increase is due to more fags and more booze. I suppose we all are drinking that little bit more as the tour progresses. Not enough to be spoken to, though, by the Mess President: the bill always details booze separately and if that section is higher than authority thinks it should be, you are invited to have a word with that gentleman. Don't know if anybody ever has received this invitation. I imagine it's a thing one would keep quiet about.

On the Mess bill against 'Silver' I find a charge of a shilling. Haven't even noticed any silver hanging around the place and would not think it has been whipped – even as a practical joke – so assume it's all been locked safely away just against this eventuality and that the shilling is for cleaning the stuff. Still at a bob a head they must have bought about a ton of Silvo or have enough trophies to stock a museum.

| | |
|---|---|
| *Op. No. 9* | *12 June 1944* |
| *Target* | Docks and 'U' boat pens at LE HAVRE |
| *A/C 'K'* | *Load* 11 x 1,000lbs.<br>2 x 500lbs. |
| *Take off* | 21:15 hrs. *Duration* 3:55 hrs |
| *Height* | 20,000ft. |
| *Flak* | Heavy and very concentrated over LE HAVRE |
| *E/A* | None sighted |

Our first daylight op (though in fact it was dark by the time we got back). We had a cover of Spitfires for it too: there seemed hundreds and hundreds of them swarming all over the place simply spoiling for a fight. You could almost visualise the Spit boys virtually begging for a squadron or two of ME109s and/or FW190s to come up and play with them. But no Luftwaffe, no nothing.

But even with all those Spits around I felt uncomfortable heading for the French coast in daylight. So, from the various conversations, did the rest of the crew. Thing is, I reckon, we've got so used, even over eight ops, to the security and comfort of the dark that we feel naked and exposed in daylight. Furtive creatures of the night, I suppose.

However, despite all that, it seemed that in no time we had homed on to Le Havre guided there – we really didn't need our maps – by the nasty stuff being flung into the sky over it. (What the Germans lack in fighters they seem to make up with their anti-aircraft batteries). The docks were easy enough to spot; not the 'U' boat pens because, obviously, they're covered in tons of concrete and, presumably, camouflaged. Had a good run-in on the docks and felt I'd got my bombs off accurately. Followed some of them down visually for a while then lost them from sight. Witnessed trail after trail of explosions across the docks: explosions which, I assumed, also took in the 'U' boat pens.

But all we dropped were 1,000 pounders plus the odd 500 pounder. Might have bashed the docks around a bit but these, I am sure, didn't even give rise to a headache for anybody in the 'U' boat pens.

There were 222 Lancs laid on for Le Havre. Which goes to show how important the pens must be regarded by our people. But I'll wager 'Butch' Harris isn't all that happy about this – that's 222 Lancs less for his Reich area bashing.

As for me, and the others in the crew, we'll settle for French docks and 'U' boat pens any time . . .

**15 June 1944**
On climbing out of the Lanc after the Le Havre raid, there was a Service Policeman waiting for us. He asked for F/O Muirhead. Wondering what was up, I indicated myself. He then pointed to a Police Constable standing, complete with bike and cycle clips, at the edge of the bay, just beside the perimeter track. 'He wants to see you, sir,' he explained. Fearing sad news from home, I went across to him. 'I'm F/O Muirhead,' I said. 'What's up?' He produced his notebook and slowly referred to it. 'Are you, sir,' he intoned, 'the possessor of a Derringer gun?' After a moment's reflection, I answered in the affirmative, to which he replied that I was guilty of a serious offence – I had no current permit for it. I nearly burst out laughing.

But by then, the dispersal 'bus was turning into the bay.

'Look, constable,' I said. 'I have to go to de-briefing now. Why not grab a cup of tea and I'll meet you after it? Only be about 15 minutes.'

He pondered for a second, no doubt contemplating whether or not I'd run away. Then he saluted his agreement.

All this watched with great interest by the crews in the 'bus. Especially by my own. And as I climbed in, dragging my parachute behind me, Vernon said: 'I hope you told him you never touched her.' There were also several other pieces of advice such as: 'Tell him she swore she was over 16' and 'If you weren't the only one she can't get you for paternity'. And so on. I told them it was about an expired gun licence. Roars of laughter at this including an observation that I was an untruthful person and born out of wedlock to boot.

But it was true. About the Derringer, I mean. This four-barrelled weapon (where the firing-pin rotates round four fixed barrels) I obtained from my Uncle Bob, who had an antique shop in Lady Lawson Street in Edinburgh – and who had the nerve to charge me a quid for it. Stationed at the RDF Unit at Bawdsey as a ground gunner at the time. Went to a gunsmith's at Felixstowe to buy ammo for it (.25 bullets), but no dice – had to have a police permit first. Was asked by the police to state the reason for the Derringer and replied: 'To shoot rabbits.' Now with that thing, even if a rabbit had peered up all four barrels, I think he would still have escaped the pot. Eventually the spring, which was in the butt, broke: as the cost of hand-fashioning a new spring was to be 30/- and as my daily rate of pay was two bob, I relegated the weapon to the foot of my kit bag and promptly forgot about it. Also about the licence.

The PC was there outside the de-briefing room, his cycle clips still in position.

'About having no gun permit, sir,' he said, 'while it's a serious offence, there is no question of preferring charges.'

At which my mind amused itself for one delightful moment on the RAF's reactions to their being deprived of my services by my being arrested on a charge of possessing an unlicenced, although unusable, Derringer, and being carted away from Wickenby. By trying hard, I did not smile.

I told the PC the score, adding that I no longer wished to keep the weapon and that he could have it for Police Funds or whatever. He thanked me gravely and accompanied me to my billet where I handed the Derringer to him. He solemnly wrote me out a receipt.

But this could only happen in England, couldn't it? (Or in Scotland, of course.) There am I having flown eight times over Occupied Europe and once over the Reich dropping immense weights of bombs, which are killing people, destroying houses, factories and so on, and with two .303 Browning machine guns in my front turret loaded and cocked and just awaiting the curling of my fingers around their triggers, and I return to find the British Constabulary 'worried' because I haven't renewed a permit for a Derringer. Wonderful!

**15 June 1944**

Game of football arranged for this afternoon. Between aircrew officers and aircrew NCOs. Horsfall, of course, wanted it to be rugby and made, to this end, quite a lot of noise, but was invited to get lost (actually expressed rather more strongly than that).

Vernon wanted it to be Yank football, but nobody knew enough about that sport: and besides nobody wanted it.

I didn't play because football leaves me cold: besides, the officers' team was over-subscribed.

Great trouble over finding a referee, an officer not being acceptable to the NCOs and a sergeant not acceptable to the officers.

Even the suggestion of a WAAF was turned down, not on the grounds of language (team language, that is: not referee) but on the grounds that she'd either be an officer or other rank.

Then, of the padres, one very wisely, I felt, was on leave; and as regards the other two, some kind of theological discussion over the capabilities of each as a whistler got under way between a group of officers and NCOs. A discussion which became so heated it's a wonder it did not lead to blows.

Truly, they would have been well advised to have arranged that match for the morning rather than for the period immediately following the closing of both bars.

Suddenly, when all seemed lost, a civilian passed by on a bike. (Don't know who he was, but he must have been authorised to be on the unit.) This fellow was immediately invited to descend from his bike and referee the game. He didn't seem too keen, but obviously deemed it would be somewhat unwise to refuse.

The game got under way with an immediate goal (which all the NCOs considered offside) by the officers followed by one (which all the officers considered offside) by the NCOs. Some airmen watching made certain comments on these goals, but fell silent on receipt of threatening looks by members of both teams.

Then somehow or another the ball became punctured. The F/S Physical Training Instructor, who considered he'd been saddled most unfairly with this match, said that, unfortunately, there were no more footballs around. Everybody knew this to be a lie. But it was a face-saver for all, including himself. Someone gravely thanked the referee for his participation and he climbed back on to his bike sadly shaking his head from side to side and muttering something we could not catch. Which was probably just as well.

| | |
|---|---|
| *Op. No. 10* | *12 June 1944* |
| *Target* | Docks at BOULOGNE |
| *A/C 'M'* | *Load* 11 x 1,000lbs.<br>4 x 500lbs. |
| *Take off* | 21:00 hrs. *Duration* 3:10 hrs. |
| *Height* | 13,000ft. |
| *Flak* | Rather light, but a few accurate clusters clinging around us over the target |
| *E/A* | None sighted |

Our second daylight op. And although the entire trip took only three hours and ten minutes from take off to landing I felt distinctly uncomfortable during all of it. Felt naked flying towards the French coast in daylight: would much have preferred to have done this in the dark. One thing comforted me a bit – and, I think, the rest: that was the weather which was very cloudy. Now and then, through a gap in the clouds, we'd spot the odd Spitfire escorting us. What a beautiful kite is that Spit; her lines are so clean, so graceful. (When I was on a pilot's training course in Arizona in 1942 *that* was what I dreamed of flying: but then, so did everybody who volunteered for pilot training). The Spit would waggle his wings at us before the clouds closed in again. Someone observed that maybe the next fighter to come out of the cloudes would be a ME109: to which Vernon retorted that, if so, *we* would be into a cloud quicker than a bat out of hell. But the next gap in the clouds revealed a flight of three Spits: which put paid to any further discussion about the Luftwaffe.

The cloud cleared sufficiently over Boulogne for me to get a decent run-in to the docks and I think I placed the eleven 1,000 pounders and the four 500s quite accurately. Then the cloud closed in like a blanket: a wonder we didn't crash into another Lanc.

Fourteen a/c missing from whole evening's and night's operations.

**Later**

Learned that in these two raids on Le Havre and Boulogne great damage was done to the German E-boats (40 knot motor torpedo boats). Hadn't appreciated that the latter was an intermediate base for the E-boats from which they'd push on to their advanced base at Le Havre in the hope that from such close quarters they'd inflict heavy damage on the Allied invasion shipping. Evidently we must have created a sort of tidal wave because all the E-boats in Le Havre harbour are reported sunk.

**Later**
Had our photo taken during de-briefing. It appeared in *Flight* magazine. Sufficiently interested to fork up 1/- to buy the mag: indeed, I think all the crew bought it (though there are hints that Dunn didn't but whipped his from the Sergeants' Mess). I wrote to 'Flight' asking for a copy and, of course offering to pay. By return, I received a very good print from Fox photos in London: no charge, and with their compliments. Very kind of them, I felt.

Crew in the photo, reading from left to right:
Sgt. Griggs (Engineer)
F/O Muirhead (Bomb aimer)
Sgt. Dunn (Wireless operator)
Sgt. Norman (Navigator)
Sgt. Cartwright (Rear gunner)
P/O Horsfall (Mid-upper gunner)
F/O Vernon (Pilot)

**16 June 1944**
We had a stowaway on our day trip to Boulogne. Imagine, a bomber off to prang Occupied Europe with a stowaway aboard! Happened like this. We were out at Dispersal hanging around the Lanc as we had a while to go before start-up. A ground crew sergeant, whom we knew by sight, approached us and casually asked if he could 'come along for the ride?' In between bursts of laughter Vernon told him no dice, none whatsoever. The sergeant said it was just a short trip (he'd know that from the fuel load; probably knew the target also) and that nothing could go wrong. Vernon replied that *everything* could go wrong and that *he* wasn't going to risk a Court Martial anyway. Horsfall said all of us could get Court Martialled for being a party to it. Supposing he (the Sergeant) got wounded, or shot down even. Oh, no, there was no chance. The NCO looked so disappointed that we all felt sorry for him; but there was no way we could agree to take him along. Then someone (and I'm not putting down on paper who it was!) observed that if we *did* ever find an unauthorised bod on board once we'd taken off we could hardly turn back. After which observation we all sort of casually drifted around to the other side of the Lanc leaving the hatch open and unguarded. When we drifted back the sergeant was nowhere to be seen. None of us 'happened' to see him as we climbed in shortly after. Oh, a weak, weak defence if it had come to charges, but in the event it didn't. When we landed the sergeant said how much he'd enjoyed himself. He hung about in the Lanc while we climbed out. And no doubt slipped unobtrusively away once we'd been driven off for de-briefing.

**16 June 1944**

At last a pause for breath. Needed too – we're all feeling a bit knackered. No wonder; we've been on the go ever since that first one on Tergnier on 31 May-1 June. Be about 7 a.m. on the first by the time we'd been de-briefed then briefing in the early evening for the Bernaville op on the 2-3 June. Again about 7 a.m. on the third by time de-briefed. Not even a short break until early evening on the fourth when briefed for the Sangatte job because we managed a training flight for a couple of hours in the afternoon before it! Off to bed about 8 a.m. on the fifth until afternoon briefing for Crisbecq after which bed at the earlier time of 7 a.m. on the sixth. Then a late afternoon briefing on that day for Acheres which permits you into your pit by about 7 a.m. on the seventh. On the eighth an evening briefing for Flers and by the time you finished with that it's after 7 a.m. on the tenth. Rest of that day off – big deal. On the eleventh late afternoon briefing for Evreux. An early 'night' there – in bed by 6.30 a.m. on the twelfth. Lengthy afternoon briefing on that day for Gelsenkirchen. Lengthier de-briefing too; it's nearly 7.30 on the thirteenth by the time the de-briefing's over. A break until the next afternoon when briefing for Le Havre. Back at the comparatively civilised hour of 1 a.m. on the fifteenth; just about the same time you'd return from a dance. Afternoon briefing the same day for Boulogne and back even sooner – just after midnight. God, you could have *gone* to a late night dance at that time. In the unlikely event of your wanting to, that is.

And now it's the sixteenth. And so far there's nothing on. Except talk about a training flight tomorrow evening. Can't object: training flights are all to the good. But it's certainly been quite hectic. However, not as hectic, I fancy, as the activities of the brown jobs in the Invasion forces who in some cases are at it 24 hours a day. and *without* a comfy bed to retire to from time to time. No, certainly nothing to complain about on my part.

Meant to record earlier that on one of the above efforts (I forget which) we flew near Dunkirk and that I found myself reflecting on how circumstances had changed since 1940. The Luftwaffe in its hundreds swarming over the beaches trying to prevent the evacuation: hardly a RAF fighter around. In their quite understandable ignorance, the squaddies assaulted quite a few RAF types on their safe return to England mouthing that the RAF had let them down, that it was nowhere to be seen. They could not know that the Spits and Hurries were fighting fiercely against the German bombers which were trying to get through to the crowded beaches and that these air battles were taking place as far distant, for example, as Lille, over 30 miles away where they could not be seen. If intercepted *over* Dunkirk the German bombers, which generally bombed from around 10,000ft. in most cases, could have wreaked complete havoc before being attacked. The interception simply had to take place well before the beaches. But, as I've noted, the harassed and scared (who wouldn't have been) soldiers crouching in the sand dunes weren't to know all that.

Different days now: us in our Lancasters flying calmly – well, relatively calmly – past those very same beaches and beaming benignly on the swarming Spitfires the pilots of which were no doubt a bit cheesed off at the fact that none of the Luftwaffe put in an appearance. Not one: and this from an Air Force which had been able to put up around 3,500 kites in its attack on Holland, Belgium, then France in formations of as many as 70 to 80 a time. Changed days indeed!

Should, perhaps, record that at a recent briefing I noticed a bod wearing a scruffy old sports jacket instead of battle-blouse. RAF blue shirt, RAF trousers, but a civvy jacket! This to help evading if shot down. And have since learned that some, while not going as far as wearing a sports jacket at briefing (which I'm sure higher authority would frown upon) take one along with them on an op. Evidently, if captured, the Germans don't treat you as a civvy if you're wearing at least *part* of your RAF uniform *and* are wearing your identity discs. Well, I don't have an old sports jacket around – and I'm certainly not going to buy one – so if I get shot down over France I'll simply have to dress off the country, so to speak. In mentioning this in the Mess, discovered that one character takes a black beret along with him – an item which I wouldn't think would be in short supply in France. And another says he's a good mind to take a *bowler* hat along. Says it would be good for a laugh if he has to bale out. Imagine descending by parachute wearing a bowler (if it stayed on, that is – which I very much doubt). God, the Germans would die laughing! No, on second thoughts I don't think they would: they'd probably regard it as particularly unfunny.

**17 June 1944**

All crews to report to the Briefing Room at 10:00 hrs: non-operational as well, so it can't be an op. For once we were there ahead of time, far less dead on it, and sat ourselves in the front row. Wing Commander Nelson, that most likeable New Zealander, popular with all, appeared accompanied by one of the Intelligence types plus a P/O bomb aimer I had never seen before. We were in the process of shuffling into what might be termed, very loosely, as some form of attention when he motioned to us to sit down again. He next informed us that we might smoke: a wry smile as he gave this permission, mainly, I think, because about half of us were smoking already. He then handed us over to the Intelligence chap. I got the impression that Winco Nelson was present mainly to ensure that this P/O – obviously the star of whatever show was going to be put on for us – was accorded a fair hearing, free from interruption, and would be able to say whatever he had to say subject to the very minimum of wisecracks.

The Intelligence Officer now introduced the P/O bomb aimer who was from some other Squadron in No. 1 Group. He explained that the P/O who had to bale out over France, was able to contact the Resistance who were instrumental in spiriting him out of France into Spain from where he was able to return to England. He was sure we would find his experiences interesting: some of us might even gain from them if we ever found ourselves in a similar position. He ignored the remark: 'Not if I can help it' which came from somewhere near us.

The P/O kicked off rather well. He had obviously spotted my bomb aimer's flying badge – he could hardly fail to do so being almost opposite me. He smiled at me, nodded, and observed: 'See you've got a moustache.'

'Enables me to keep a stiff uper lip in a crisis,' I informed him.

'Also helps to strain the gallons of beer he knocks back,' amplified Horsfall.

'Well, I also used to have a moustache,' continued the P/O, unruffled.

'How interesting!' murmured someone.

Our guest pressed on: 'But I shaved it off in France.'

'During you parachute descent?' This from the back of the room.

Winco Nelson's deepening frown rose with him. 'All right, gentlemen,' he ordered. 'Half-wit time over. We'll now listen in silence.' He sat down again and nodded at our visitor.

'Yes, I shaved it off. Because young Frenchmen don't as a rule wear moustaches. For *you* to sport one might attract attention.' He looked at me again. 'Might be a good idea to tuck a razor and a spot of soap into your blouse pocket.'

I nodded at him and determined to do just that.

No interruptions from now on: all listened intently. It was odd how this bod's experiences coincided, in the beginning anyway, with the earlier Intelligence lecture. Dusk falling when the crew had to bale out: he landed in a field and hid his parachute and harness as best he could. He then started walking. Dark now and curfew time so he hid whenever he saw a vehicle approach. Eventually he came to a village and made his way to the church. There was a house beside it which he took to be the priest's. He knocked at the door. When the priest opened it he started to explain, in what he described to us as school-boy French, that he was an RAF airman who'd been shot down. He got no further than that: the priest informed him that he couldn't assist him in any way, that he should surrender to the local *gendarme*. He added, helpfully, just before he slammed the door, that this gentleman lived just along the street there. The P/O walked off, but in the opposite direction: he told us that, as he did so, he could discern a slight movement of the curtains. A short distance away was a barn: he entered it, saw a pile of straw, burrowed into it and immediately fell asleep.

It was the slap on the face which awakened him: and he found himself staring at a knife held uncomfortably close to his throat.

Yes, so far, exactly as the Intelligence Officer had forecast in that earlier lecture of his. And then the penny dropped. Honestly, at times I think I'm remarkably slow on the uptake. It would be a month or so ago when our bomb aimer lecturer arrived back in England. And there he would be accorded a massive and intensive de-briefing, every small detail, no matter apparently how trivial, being recorded.

All of that written down, commented on, etc. and then issued to Intelligence Officers on operational units. Yes, what the IO had been recounting to us earlier had been based on this bod's experiences.

On murmuring my 'discovery' to Horsfall, I was rewarded with just one word: 'Balls.' So I fell silent and continued listening.

The Resistance people had, of course, been told of his presence by the priest (whom, he said, he never saw again). They tied his wrists together behind his back, put a blindfold on him and thereafter took him on a long, stumbling walk. When the blindfold eventually was removed he found himself in a farmhouse kitchen. Still bound, he was thrust onto a chair. He opened his mouth to protest, but shut it again when a hand was raised to slap him. Shortly after, a tall, thin individual appeared. In quite good English he asked him for his name, number and rank, which he gave. Next he asked him his Squadron number and base. The P/O refused to give this. The slap from the interrogator was vicious. And it set the would-be evader off on a swearing spree which, he confessed to us, amazed even himself. This, curiously enough, didn't fetch another slap. Instead, once the profanities and blasphemies had tailed off, his interrogator explained that he was a school-teacher and that it was up to *him* to decide whether or not their prisoner was a German *agent-provacateur*. This was too much for our P/O friend – he burst out laughing. But stopped it in mid-stream when informed that, if he was, it would certainly be no laughing matter for him. The school-teacher went on to explain what had happened when the Germans had dropped English-speaking men dressed in RAF uniform. And, after it, once more asked for Squadron and station. Which was given. Then he asked for rough details of home town, which was Manchester. These also were given. The school-teacher then disappeared. He didn't come back for two days during which the P/O continued to remain closely guarded.

On his return, the interrogator had only two questions to ask.

And they concerned tram routes in Manchester. Clever, that: most unlikely for a German to know details of tram routes in and around Manchester. I didn't take notes but, if it had been me, the home town would have been Edinburgh and the two (comparative) questions would have been on the lines of the following:

1. Q. Does the No. 12 tram still run to Musselburgh?
   *Correct answer.* No. It never did. It terminates at Joppa.
2. Q. When does the last tram pass the Caledonian Hotel at night and what is its number? (Failing which, its depot).
   *Correct answer.* About 11:40 p.m. And it's the No. 4 (heading for the Portobello depot).

Quite clever really, the Resistance getting a wireless signal back to England saying they'd picked up a character claiming to be P/O so-and-so, whose home town was Manchester and asking what questions to put to him: and receiving those over the space of a couple of days.

But no so clever, I suppose, if the escapee concerned was one of those persons who wouldn't know his home-town tram service numbers even if tattooed all over himself . . .

However, the answers satisfied his interrogator: aided, he surmised, by the fact that, when slapped, none of his outraged and profane outbursts had been in German. All friends now, bonds removed, food and wine. He was kept there another day and then passed down the line. He explained to us how careful he was not to remember names of people or of places so that, if the worst came to the worst, he would not be able to reveal them: also that, while he divested himself of his battle-blouse (in favour of a scruffy old jacket supplied courtesy of the Resistance) he retained his RAF trousers and blue shirt; this latter, he explained, to avoid being accused of wearing civvies.

I found all this very interesting, as I'm sure all the other crews did also.

But what was even *more* interesting to absolutely everyone in that Briefing Room was the P/O bomb aimer's *finale*. Really, I'm sure he had worked hard on it, honing away until he had it polished to perfection. He informed us that the end of the French line, for him anyway, was a brothel in Paris. That, he intimated, was where the Resistance lodged him until he could be put on the train to Perpignan – a Paris brothel.

'Spare us absolutely no details, please,' came crisply from the back.

'Any photos?' asked another.

'Right, right,' ordered Winco Nelson, making a downward motion with his hand.

And indeed, no details were spared. Our visitor was listened to in complete silence as he described day-to-day and night-to-night life in the brothel. There were six girls there, he explained, some pretty, others less so. Three had the clap and they were reserved for the Germans (outburst of cheering at this choice piece of information): of the remaining three, two were reserved for their French regular customers (more but rather subdued cheering this time). And the sixth, who was also by far the prettiest, was – and here our P/O paused for effect – reserved for *him*. (No cheering this time: only an observation from the body of the room that some bastards seemed to have all the bloody luck.)

Some nods and jealous murmurs as he explained, that, whenever the German MPs raided the place, he would hop into bed with this girl and try to arrange his timing so that when the MPs burst into the bedroom he was, in his own words, 'performing'. The MPs would make what he took to be lewd noises, but would take no further action such as asking for papers and so on. He was kept in this brothel for about two weeks. He was then taken by the Resistance to the station to take the train to Perpignan. Now he came to his *pièce de résistance*.

'I was told,' he said, 'that after Perpignan I'd have to make Spain by climbing the Pyrenees.' He paused. 'Christ, after a fortnight in that knocking shop, far less the Pyrenees, I could hardly climb the steps up into that f.....g train.'

This brought the house down, no doubt as it had at the other squadrons he'd visited. And Winco Nelson suddenly found something of great interest to him in an adjacent wall-map.

The IO quietened the applause by inviting questions. But as those were all about the brothel and nothing else, he quickly thanked our visitor and drew the proceedings to a close.

Rather long the above, I know. And really only but faintly connected with my diary. But worth, I think, writing up.

PS I should have noted that this P/O bomb aimer can never fly over Germany or Occupied Europe again. It is RAF policy not to allow anyone who has been in contact with the Resistance to do so. This because the Germans almost certainly know of his name and that he was spirited out of France and into Spain by the Resistance. If he flew operationally again and they got their hands on him they'd torture him until he revealed everything he knew about his earlier encounters with the Resistance. Evidently second time around and no holds are barred by the Germans when they have the chance of exterminating as much of the French Resistance movement as they can accomplish.

Should maybe also note that I don't believe his spiel about three with the clap being reserved for the Germans. The Germans are not exactly stupid – they'd fasten on right away to where their people were picking up a dose (though I've heard that catching VD in the German Forces is such a serious offence that many with it go to extraordinary lengths to keep the fact quiet). Think, actually, he'd made that up; or that someone at the brothel had been having him on.

**18 June 1944**
Stood-down now. For quite a bit, it seems, because the weather has clamped.

So we had a Mess 'do' last night. And after about 3 pints we decided that Vernon would perform the 'black footprints' effort. Vernon wasn't all that enthusiastic but he's slightly built whereas I'm not and Horsfall, being a Yorkshire rugby player, is on the burly side (surprisingly, though, how easily he slides into his mid-upper gun turret). Anyway, we grab Vernon, remove his shoes. Someone fetches a basin into which we pour beer and, strictly according to recipe, mix thoroughly with soot from the ante-room chimney. Into the brew goes Vernon's stockinged feet. Then Horsfall grabs him by one side while I do likewise the other. We lift him. Vernon now accepts the inevitable and jerks both his feet up. We then 'walk' him up one wall, across the ceiling and down the other wall leaving a dirty trail of black footprints. Vernon quite enjoys all this and when 'encore' is shouted we do the same again but from the opposite end of the ante-room. Then someone says anything the Yanks can do the English can do better. So some pilot from Devon takes his place and, supported and guided by two navigators, leaves his footprints on walls and ceilings. Much hilarity.

**Added later** We were all fined 15/6d for the cost of cleaning the walls. That is, everybody who was in the ante-room that night. The Mess Secretary simply added the 15/6d to our Mess bills. How he knew exactly who was in the ante-room God alone knows. (Some call him the Wickenby Gestapo.) Must record something about the Mess Secretary when I get the time. Will do so tomorrow, if still stood down.

**18 June 1944**
Am down in the Intelligence Section for this entry. A wonderful place to do research – they have nearly every publication under the sun (every *war* publication, that is; despite popular demand they don't have *Men Only*, *Lilliput* and so on, presumably because, if they had, aircrew would spend more time on them and less on the official efforts).

Purpose was to compare losses on our first German raid (Gelsenkirchen) with those incurred on some earlier German targets. And, almost mesmerised by the sheer awfulness of it, I found myself drawn back again to the dreadful night of 30 March 1944 and Nuremberg, details of which I noted in this book on 3 June. Mind-numbing stuff compared with our Gelsenkirchen op where, out of the 275 who took part, only 17 were missing. (Even so, that's 119 bods either killed or in the bag.)

Also renewed my feeling of gratitude that I wasn't on ops at that time, that my entry to the scene was delayed because of that grumbling appendix when training on Ansons up in Dumfries in August of last year. As I think I recorded earlier, without this enforced delay I might well have been involved in that Nuremberg disaster. Just hope that luck stays.

**18 June 1944**

A bomb aimer shot a most terrible line in the Mess this evening about his always being the only bombs which were dropped absolutely spot-on, no matter the flak, no matter how much harassment by night-fighters. It was decided, most solemnly, that a de-bagging operation was called for. He made for the door, but a very crafty piece of interception by myself and another bomb aimer quickly brought him to the deck. In the middle of the de-bagging session in walked the WAAF Intelligence Officer who (no pun intended) de-briefed us after the Boulogne op. She showed an interest in the proceedings and gave no signs of going into reverse. Until Horsfall informed her that she was next. At which she took off at maximum revs . . .

**19 June 1944**

Walking round to Sandy Mansfield's office – he's Bombing Leader – this morning when a Group Captain emerged from SHQ. I cocked him up one. By my standards a smart-enough salute (though I suppose it would have brought anyone in the Scots Guards out in a rash). Had just passed him when I heard: 'Flying Officer, just a moment, please.'

Thought the salute mustn't have met with much approval so put a bit more into my next effort.

He gave a wry sort of smile and asked: 'Could you give me some information, please?' I assured him that I would be delighted to do so. To which he continued: 'What is that you have upon your head?'

'My hat, sir,' I replied. (Well, what else can you say, especially as you have a pretty good idea of what's coming next?)

'Thank you, Flying Officer,' he continued. 'I just wanted to know, that's all.' And off he went.

Of course, this was but one example of the cavalier disregard of rules by operational air-crew. Orders every now and then that hat-bands must not be removed from caps. We are told that, minus hat-bands, our hats look slovenly and sloppy. Which I admit they do. But we like our hats that way despite once being informed that we gave the appearance of being broken-down 'bus conductors. Most of us have long-since flung away those 'stiffeners' anyway. And when we buy a new cap – which is not often – the first thing we do is remove the band.

I always take my hat with me on ops (which doesn't do it any good). If I ever have to parachute out it'll go with me, stuffed inside my battle-blouse. And if, after that, I end up in the bag, I'm going to walk in there with that hat upon my head. Minus one hat-band of course . . .

**19 June 1944**

Again, not operational material, but a number of things I feel like noting all the same.

(a) Those letters from Edinburgh informing me of the death of school chums who started flying on ops just about the same time as I did. Rather not hear about their buying it. In any case nearly all seem to have got the chop. I try to think up names of some still alive, but cannot recall any. Don't tell me I'm the only one left . . .

(b) On one of the raids over Germany I began to wonder whether an old school chum, Dougie Jones, who was captured at St. Valerie, was maybe in a POW camp below me. I would hope not near where my bombs landed. Difficult to write to Dougie, (I have, of course, to put my Portobello address on the POW letter) because I can't tell him where I am or what I'm doing. And it's not very clever to say much about food because we understand POWs are on pretty short rations. So letters are mainly about swing bands and films: and maybe the odd pre-war recollection.

(c) Why does 'Butch' Harris never visit his Bomber Squadrons? We'd be delighted to see him. Most of us don't know whether we like him or not. They say he's not a very friendly type, that he's dedicated himself to laying Germany absolutely flat. It's a worthwhile dedication: the bastards deserve all they've been getting and what they're going to get. Wonder if they still support Hitler just as much as they did before all that destruction started descending from the skies on to their cities.

**19 June 1944**

The things some of the bods get up to! With no flying tonight, the bar was quite busy. After it closed some stayed on in the ante-room, having ordered a few pints before the shutters went up and being determined to finish them. About midnight someone said: 'What about building a pyramid then?' Must confess this was a new one on me. Evidently not to others (chaps who'd been operational longer than I had, I think) who set about the operation with great expertise. And this was to balance one of the Mess chairs on two legs then build upwards and outwards with the rest until a whole pile of chairs was balanced delicately on this single 'base chair'. A rope was then produced: one end was tied to the ante-room door, the other to this finely-balanced 'base chair'. It was only then that I appreciated that the ante-room door opened *outwards*.

All then depart by a window.

**20 June 1944**

This morning the first officer – none of us – to approach the ante-room door found it somewhat stiff. He pulled. It didn't open so he pulled harder. It opened and this massive pile of chairs collapsed all over the place, two of them going through a window.

For once, the Mess Secretary didn't know who'd been engaged in this building etc. exercise for a notice appeared in the Mess that afternoon inviting all who had participated to append their names to it so that they might pay their share of the damage done. As far as I know, everyone who was there signed. It'll only be about five bob each anyway. And as one bod said: 'Ah well, I'll probably get the chop before he can collect, so why worry?' Personally, I'll be only too happy to be around to fork up that five bob!

**20 June 1944**

Vernon looked into my room today. Expressed surprise that I wasn't writing. 'You always seem to be scribbling away in that goddamn book of yours,' he observed. 'Hope you've not been putting down any shit against the name of Vernon.' I said I hadn't. Not yet anyway. Asked if I never got tired of it. I answered that I didn't, that I enjoyed it. He advised me to keep on enjoying it because as sure as fate I'd never be able to finish the effing thing, not the way the losses seemed to be mounting. Then he tossed me a carton of Chesterfields adding that he knew the Scots always liked something for nothing. I congratulated him on being so well informed adding that if he accompanied me to the bar, which was now open, I'd buy him a half pint. Grinning that he knew bloody well I wouldn't rise to a *full* pint, he said OK. Felt at that stage we were beginning to get to know each other rather better. After a couple of jars I asked him to give me his mother's address.

'So you can write to her, supposing you make it and I don't, telling her what a brave guy her son was, eh?' he added.

'No. It's just that my mother can get some wizard shortbread in Crawfords in Edinburgh,' I replied. 'She's got an oppo who works there. Give me your mother's address; I'll send it to mine and ask her to post her a box.'

Vernon said OK, later. He made no attempt to write it down there and then. I knew he never will.

Horsfall came in shortly after. He looked enquiringly first at Vernon then at me. The bar steward asked, 'Yes, sir?' I said, 'A pint for the gentleman, please.'

Horsfall grabbed it. 'Christ!' he observed, 'wonders will never bloody well cease.' He sunk most of it in one noisy gulp.

'What made you call him a gentleman?' asked Vernon, indicating the dribble on Horsfall's chin.

'I'm going round the bend, that's why,' I informed him.

**21 June 1944**

With no flying tonight – none whatsoever due to duff weather – a sort of spontaneous boozing session gets under way in the Mess. A Mess Rule, 'to be strictly observed' and never mind the split-infinitive, is that no Mess member is to stand treat. Sensible enough: the Service just trying to ensure you don't fling away your 13/6d a day (if P/O) or your 15/6d a day (if F/O) on buying booze for other bods. Yes, to be strictly observed: and strictly we ignore it. Generally we ignore, in a cavalier fashion, most Rules and most Regulations. Except for flying ones, that is. After a few pints someone announces that we have approached recitation time. A WAAF officer, who has just arrived at Wickenby, and who, from her accent simply must be a product of Roedean, places her lady-like sherry on a table and starts clapping her hands and at the same time making anticipatory, gushing noises. She gets frowned at by all: and I take it upon myself to inform her that I have reason to believe that the first recitation might well be 'Twas on the good ship Venus' and that accordingly she might prefer to take off. This thoughtful and well-meant advice she rejects somewhat haughtily. And as she does so some pilot, whose name I don't know, gets the first verse airborne:

'Twas on the good ship Venus
By Christ, you should have seen us
The figure-head was a whore in bed
The mast a rampant penis.'

They breed them tough at Roedean; the lass stands her ground. Her smile, however, is not quite so toothy. And she gulps at her sherry as the second verse lurches under way:

'The cabin boy's name was Sam
He *was* a saucy nipper
He filled his arse with broken glass
And circumcised the skipper.'

I say to the WAAF: 'It gets slightly vulgar after this.'

She takes off. Quite smartly, her smile fading rapidly into the past.

Eventually the good ship Venus founders. So next we start singing: 'The Ball o' Kirriemuir'. A tall navigator seems to know more verses than all of us put together. Vernon, being a Yank, has never even *heard* this subtle piece of folk-lore before and is rather bemused. I inform him that this account of a dance in Fife, Scotland, which ended up in a frantic free-for-all sexual orgy, basically is true (as it is although perhaps enlarged upon somewhat by numerous Service choirs): to which he replies shit, pull the other and whose round is it, by the way? I tell him it's Horsfall's: but that worthy is too absorbed in the intimate details of yet another incident which it is alleged took place at Kirriemuir to even *think* about ordering a round.

We get to what must surely be around the thirtieth verse (which is the one where Aggie McCafferty had us all in fits, a-jumping from the mantelpiece and bouncing on her – guess whats?), when the Mess Secretary strides in and immediately closes the bar. He is awarded the Hitler salute together with cries of 'Mein Fuhrer' from some, a two-fingered salute from a couple and, from one, the offer of a dance. This he refuses. He bestows on each of us an intense glare which suggests that he's recording mentally all our names as against any Mess damage and strides off again.

We all repair slowly to our billets.

| | |
|---|---|
| *Op. No. 11* | *22 June 1944* |
| *Target* | Robot-bomb installations at WISSANT |
| *A/C 'B'* | *Load* 18x500lbs. |
| *Take off* | 14:12 hrs. *Duration* 3:15 hrs. |
| *Height* | 14,800ft. |
| *Flak* | Light but determined. None too near us. Some crews saw a Lanc shot down, though. Crew evidently managed to bale out |
| *E/A* | None sighted |

Another daylight op. Target sighted visually: followed my bombs all the way down and saw them explode. Hate to admit it, but I found that a most fascinating sight. Cover of Spitfires and Lightnings.

A beautiful summer's afternoon with France below us seemingly stretching on and on and looking so delightful, so peaceful, so welcoming. I must visit that country (but not, I hope, by courtesy of the Germans!) Yes, if I make it, I'm going there after the war. God, what we're all going to do after the war! Chaps in the Mess sometimes talk about after it's over: but only half-heartedly – got to survive the damn thing first.

Lots of Spits, plus some Lightnings, swarming about, spoiling for a fight. Would be a brave FW190 or ME109 to venture into the air. Sometimes I think these fighter boys, in the absence of the Luftwaffe, would be more than prepared to take each other on . . .

Was able to spot quite easily the sort of ramp-like things from which these robot bombs are launched. Camouflaged, I know, but even from about 15,000ft. could be identified. Odd, but you could make out the outlines of paths to them from the edges of the surrounding fields. Would have credited the Germans with more thoroughness than that – paths across grass made by feet stick out a mile when viewed from the air. Especially on a clear sunny day such as this.

With a straight bombing run, not bothered too much by the flak, was able to straddle the site: think I got two of the ramps. There were only three or four Lancs on this one and all approached the site from different directions pretty well, as far as I could make out, blanketing it.

I then suggested to Vernon that we go down to strafe the flak posts. He thought this might be a good idea: so did the others, except Dunn and Norman, both of whom declared we'd gone round the bend. He put the Lanc into a steep dive pulling up at about 1,000ft. We headed for the nearest flak post which, very surprisingly, was barely camouflaged. I held off as long as possible then opened up with my twin Brownings, keeping the trigger pressed and taking a chance on their jamming. As we passed the post, Vernon banked slightly giving Horsfall the opportunity to bring his two Brownings to bear. Then, once over it, Cartwright, from his rear turret, let fly with his four guns. Vernon next pulled her round and we did the same from the opposite direction. As we did so, we noticed another Lanc similarly on the strafe nearby.

Must give the German gunners their due: no running away – they kept on firing all the time, even when we were bearing down on them with guns blazing.

I don't know for sure whether we knocked out those flak posts or not, our guns firing, of course, only .303 bullets. And, naturally, we didn't mention this little bit of what might be termed 'free enterprise' at de-briefing. Certainly not: they view that kind of thing somewhat sourly – you might lose them one of their precious Lancasters. (And just *think* what 'Butch' would say were he to learn that he'd lost one of his heavies – grudgingly diverted from the bombing of Germany – as a result of unauthorised activities over France. God, he'd have had a flaming fit!)

**22 June 1944**

Harking back to the bravery of these Luftwaffe AA gunners at Wissant, I cannot help but compare with the cowardice of myself, plus that of a hairdresser from Nottingham named Holland, when in a rather similar position back in 1940.

Awaiting air-crew training, I had been posted as a ground-gunner to RAF Bawdsey, near Ipswich. An RDF station (later to be called radar). In a dug-out on the edge of a cliff with two machine guns. Some Stukas around and one appearing out of the clouds and decided to bomb Bawdsey. Started firing at the dive-bomber but, as he went into his dive, with his syren screaming, we thought better of it and flung ourselves down behind the sandbags. Once he'd passed overhead, we came out and resumed firing (forgetting his rear-gunner's Spandeau, which spat briefly at us).

No excuse to say that, anyway, his bomb fell in a wood.

And no excuse to say that the machine guns we had were 1914-1918 Lewis efforts off Camels etc. and, with no air-flow to cool them, jammed after about 10 rounds in any case.

No, no excuses there: none whatever.

But have come a long way since then. It's *my* turn now. Feel I've got some of my own back with that Wissant machine-gunning.

**Note: 23 June 1944**

Stood down. Our a/c 'B' for Baker, which was recently given to us as our 'own' Lanc (which accounts for the fact that we had only made one trip in it) was allocated to a P/O Jeffrey and crew for their second op. Don't know what the target was: being stood down, we didn't bother to find out. Looks as if that second op was also their last – 'B' for Baker reported missing with no word of crew. Next day still no word so that's definitely curtains for 'B' for Baker and seven inexperienced air crew members. One can only hope they've ended up as POW.

Odd how casual one gets about referring to some pilot and crew who've bought it. I wrote above: 'a P/O Jeffrey and crew'. I cannot recall a P/O Jeffrey. We may have met; we may not have. For all I know, I could have been sitting next to him when we were eating our pre-op bacon and eggs: or had a pint with him at the bar. Generally, you don't ask anybody his name and he does not seek yours. You never get very friendly with any particular chap, treating all as casual acquaintances. Also being flippant towards them.

This flippancy demonstrated when a P/O navigator, on his return from leave, asked around about some other navigator. When told he had gone missing and was presumed killed, his only observation was: 'The bastard! He owes me half-a-crown.'

We are to get a brand new Lanc which will be arriving from the factory tomorrow. We are looking forward to getting it and hope the weather won't delay its arrival. Because that's all that *can* delay it – when Avro say 'tomorrow' they mean just that.

**24 June**

In a way got my own back on Vernon today. Had known for sure he'd never get around to giving his mother's address. So I 'phoned my own mother and asked her to get the shortbread and send it to me. She said she would. But she then wrote saying this wasn't possible as it simply wasn't made now. So, out of her hoarded rations, she had made a cake of it herself.

I took her shortbread to Vernon, who was in his room reading a book. After expressing surprise at his progressing beyond 'the funnies', I gave him the shortbread.

'What's this for?' He eyed the package suspiciously. Resisting the temptation of a vulgar reply, I informed him that it was shortbread for his mother and that I hoped he would send it to her and not woof the entire bloody lot himself adding that I wouldn't be surprised if he did.

He nodded his thanks, rose, put it in a locker. In the same movement he produced a bottle. 'Fancy a drop of this?' he invited, not showing me the label.

'What is it?' I asked.

'Whisky. Bourbon,' he replied.

Dreadful stuff,' I informed him. 'Not in the same class as Scotch.'

'But you'll take a dram all the same, eh?' he smiled, producing two glasses.

'Didn't know you knew the meaning of the word "dram",' I nodded. 'But make it a small one.'

'A small one is what you were getting anyway,' he said, pouring out two measures which by no means could have been described as small.

We said cheers to each other and were sitting there sipping away when, after the lightest and briefest of knocks, the door opened and in strode Horsfall.

'Jesus H. Christ!' ejaculated Vernon. 'I might have known: that bugger has an in-built radar set that can detect free booze at a hundred yards.'

'All I looked in for was to ask you if you wanted to come for a walk,' explained Horsfall.

'A likely story!' As he spoke, Vernon poured him a large measure also.

But that was it. No drinking session ahead. So often you start what is to be a solitary drink and, almost before you know it, have emptied the bottle. Not much joy in that if you're flying, especially operationally. We finished our drinks and Vernon put the Bourbon away.

'What about that walk, then?' asked Horsfall.

'Stuff it!' invited Vernon.

'You, maybe?' Horsfall had turned to me.

My invitation was worded exactly as had been Vernon's.

Wouldn't mind some leave if this duff weather's going to continue, but I suppose they can't afford to let us very far from Wickenby with so much going on across the Channel: just in case the weather clears.

The Mess Secretary I referred to recently: don't even know his name; he's simply referred to as 'Mess Sec'. Aberdeen, I think from his accent. A left-over from WW I. But with pilot's wings. On more than one occasion he has referred to us (the aircrew, that is) as 'the biggest, and worst, shower of shit it has ever been my misfortune to encounter'. But when he conveys this view of his to us we notice it's never within the hearing of ground staff officers or the Mess staff. Generally I think all feel that in WW I he and his oppos behaved rather like we do now. And when it comes to asking him for the odd bottle of whisky to take on leave he's really only too happy to oblige, but at the same time accusing you of only wanting it to flog on the black market.

On the subject of the black market I reckon Cliff, my batman, is involved in it – can get you practically anything. (Pompous to call him 'my' batman: I share him with about another four bods. All he does is make your bed and tidy your room: if you want to polish your buttons, for example, you have to do that yourself. As a consequence of sharing a batman I received what is called a 'hard-lying allowance': forget exactly how much, but I think it's about two bob a day). Cliff's not supposed to carry out duties like pressing your uniform, but he does – and you slip him something. He even got me a whistle to replace the one I'd lost. You wear this whistle attached to your blouse collar. It's for use if you find yourself in the drink and the Air/Sea Rescue types are around. Naturally, you blow it to attract their attention. You'd really have to be in a dinghy at the time: wouldn't be much joy in trying to swim and blow your whistle simultaneously . . .

High time that weather cleared. I'm writing too much about non-operational stuff. No more in this diary until our next op.

| | |
|---|---|
| *Op. No. 12* | *25 June 1944* |
| *Target* | Robot-plane installations at FLERS |
| *A/C 'V'* | *Load* 18 x 500lbs. |
| *Take off* | 01:30 hrs. *Duration* 3:35 hrs. |
| *Height* | 13,000ft. |
| *Flak* | On the light side |
| *E/A* | None sighted |
| *S/Ls* | A very wide belt right round the installations. Saw a number of Lancs coned by them. Coned ourselves too but we soon corkscrewed out into the dark |

When flying near London on our way to the French coast saw a couple of those robot-planes heading towards the City. Of course, we were going one way and they heading in the opposite direction so, what with our combined speeds, it was really only a fleeting glance we had. Each of these robots was being picked up by S/Ls then transferred from one cluster of them to the other. A lot of light flak going up at them: but nothing like the flak that is hosed up over Germany. Suppose there are Mosquitos around too being guided to these things by the S/Ls.

Anyway, we continued on our way to Flers. There being quite a number of Lancs on this op, the site was thoroughly plastered. Wondered if the two we saw near London had been launched from there. Must be terrible to be at the receiving end when one of these robots plunges down. They tell us that each is, in effect, a very heavy bomb, which is probably why we're diverted on to attacking installations like those at Flers.

An easy one this. Hope there are many more like it: and my hope isn't the only one around . . .

Must note that this was our first in our new Lanc, 'V' for Victor. She's beautiful and already I've fallen in love with her. So, I think, has Vernon. Not so sure about the rest: to them she's just a kite. When I first climbed into her I was reminded of a friend in Edinburgh who'd just bought a new car (a Ford Popular: cost £100 – his old man was comparatively rich and gave it to him for his birthday. But a hundred quid – some money that). From this new car came that exciting smell of new paint, new rubber, new leather. *That* was the smell I experienced with my first sniff of 'V' for Victor.

As for her performance: exquisite. Those Rolls-Royce Merlins don't roar; they sing. No country in the world has an engine in the same class as the Merlin. Not even the Germans with their Mercedes-Benz.

'V' for Victor also has the latest model of *Gee* (wonder how much all these devices cost – must be a packet). Can't really describe this technically, but it's based on three ground transmitters all linked up together and radiating a series of pulses which you pick up on a screen: you then read off these pulses with reference to a special *Gee* map and can thus fix position. This has contributed greatly to the accuracy of our bombing raids. True, once we started using it the Germans weren't long in setting up powerful jamming stations all over Occupied Europe with the result that *Gee* now isn't all that use once you get inland and away from the coast. But you can still get a good reading before you enter enemy territory and this helps to keep right on track and therefore in the middle of the bomber stream. It's the navigator's task to operate *Gee.* Have had a go at it myself, but Norman's the more expert. Personally, I prefer to get an accurate fix as a result of good, old-fashioned map reading, but that isn't always possible. It's in cases like that when *Gee* is a quite terrific navigational aid.

**26 June 1944**

In Lincoln today bumped into an old friend. Tony McColl, who had trained with me as a bomb aimer at No. 7 Bombing and Gunnery School at Paulson, Manitoba. Like me, a failed pilot from America. He's with the Pathfinders and doesn't rate his chances very highly. We'd met at Paulson, which, quite frankly, is at the arse end of the Province. A hick town where nothing ever happens. And where the RCMP, if one can believe the locals, are nothing but dodgers from military service: certainly they didn't endear themselves to us when, on one occasion, they arrested some Aussie trainees for throwing snowballs in the street. You couldn't blame the Aussies – they'd never seen snow before; but certainly you could blame these so-called 'Mounties' for actually arresting them.

We discussed those Battle aircraft in which we'd trained at Paulson. At that time neither of us had known their terrible history at the beginning of the war. And Tony grimaced at the thought of trying to fend off an ME109 from that open rear-cockpit with one Vickers Gas Operated machine gun. We concluded how lucky we were being able to fly in ultra-modern kites like the Lanc: also by reflecting on the bravery of our predecessors who flew those dreadful Battles. Especially as the gunner was usually a tradesman who was granted the rank of LAC by virtue of being a part-time air gunner: and was also granted something like an extra shilling a day for thus volunteering. Seems quite unbelievable looking back.

Tony and I exchanged addresses. But neither will write: we made polite noises, but we both knew that.

In a pub later had a chat with a couple of Poles. I had heard of the hatred the Poles have for the Germans, but until I met up with these two hadn't really appreciated the depth and intensity of it. They are on Lancs and consider every night they're not bombing Germany and killing Germans to be a dead loss. I suppose I too would have developed such a hatred for the Germans if we had been occupied by them and had suffered atrocities similar to those committed in Poland. Those two Poles consider the Russians to be just as evil and seem to hate them just as much. No actual hatred for the French, but don't appear to have much respect for them. They like the English, they say. But they seem particularly attracted to the Scots, having been stationed in Scotland for a while. One of them intimates his intention of returning there after the war. He is engaged to a Scots girl and wants to settle in the Borders.

Found those Poles interesting, but regretfully had to leave: some airmen at the far end of the bar and a nearby group of soldiers making remarks about 'Brylcream Boys'. Possible trouble, so better beat it.

**27 June 1944**

Being stood down becomes boring if you're not detailed for a flying exercise or a lecture or whatever. Regarding the 'whatever', some bright spark had the clever idea that a spot of exercise would do wonders for us all and, accordingly, the Tannoy ordered air crew, operational and otherwise, to report outside the gym suitably attired in PT gear of singlet, shorts and gym shoes. Which presented two problems: (a) that very few, if any, of us still possessed these items, most having ditched them long, long ago and (b) none had any intention of taking part anyway. None from our Mess, that is, other than Horsfall. And the more I think of it the more I am convinced that he was the evil person behind it all: he is a right keep-fit maniac and is always nattering away how all of us need much more exercise. In the event, Horsfall was the only officer who turned up. I believe three sergeants also put in an appearance, but that was not to take part in the proceedings; they were there, they anticipated, to watch a gaggle of shivering officers dressed in singlets and shorts doing all sorts of exercises while they commented on knobbly knees and various other physical shortcomings. Anyway, all they got was Horsfall; plus, of course, the PT sergeant and his cronies. After about 15 minutes of running-on-the-spot, touching toes and various other kinds of self-inflicted discomfort, Horsfall, now getting completely and joyfully into his stride, bawled out that a cross-country would be just the thing with which to finish off the session and charged off, the PT chap and his two side-kicks following. (Sgt. Dunn told me afterwards that the PT sergeant admitted on his return that, with Horsfall, he'd bitten off more than he could chew and that he was, in his own words, 'completely buggered'.)

By the time Horsfall returned from his cross-country – which, from the time he took, must have covered a goodly part of Lincolnshire – the bar was opened and Vernon and I were having our lunch-time pint. He looked us up and down and referred to us as lazy sods. But nevertheless he sunk the pint I bought him at the same time remarking that *that* was about the only exercise Vernon and I took – lifting our right arms. I am beginning to like Horsfall a lot. His first name is Ted.

After lunch, some off to their billets either to read or to have a kip, depending, no doubt, on how many pints knocked back before it. But most hang around the ante-room. Some are awaiting their turn for the *Daily Mirror* to see how many clothes Jane has removed that day, or, more likely, the previous evening. The most popular daily in the Mess, the *Mirror*, but it's because of Jane, certainly nothing else. The most popular 'Sunday' is the *News of the World*. Funny, it's referred to as a 'Sunday' but if you're in a remote part of England or Scotland you get the mid-week edition which *arrives* on the Saturday sometime. Anyway, no matter when it's actually printed, you have it on the Sunday morning and, if you're quick off the mark, can grab one of the six copies the Mess receives, so that, when the inevitable reference is made to some scoutmaster or some vicar whose activities have exceeded their official remits to such an extent that they are now about to depart from the social scene for varying periods of time, you are able to take part in the ensuing discussion fully genned up. Heady, stimulating stuff.

Of course, there's the *Express* too. And the *Mail*. Also, among others, the *Herald*, which virtually nobody reads. Then there's *The Times*. You have to be careful when you're reading *The Times*. Especially if it's in the afternoon when the effect of these pre-lunch drinks has not quite worn off. More especially still if you're holding it wide open with both arms fully stretched. Because then you cannot see what is happening in front of you. And, fortified by these pre-lunch drinks, someone is creeping towards you on all fours with a box of matches. Next, your *Times* is a sheet of flame and you're on your feet, cursing and swearing while you stamp it out.

Only two copies of *The Times* are taken, the Mess Secretary reckoning, quite correctly, that air-crew intellect is such that very few would be able to comprehend a newspaper which used any words comprising more than about five letters: and wouldn't be interested anyway unless it was mostly made up of photographs. On one unfortunate occasion, both copies became the basis of quite a sizeable pyrotechnic display. Which gave rise to a written protest to the Mess President by an officer in Accounts or Equipment – I forget which – who set great score on reading his *Times* every evening when he knocked off duty. His grievance was most justified. As a result, a notice went up on the board outside the ante-room intimating that no more *Times* were to be set alight. It didn't mention any other newspapers so presumably we still have the *Express*, *Mail*, etc. on which to practise our fire-raising skills . . .

Also, and this applies at all times in the ante-room, except perhaps in the morning, you must not doze off with your legs stretched out in front of you. Asking for a couple of lighted matches to be dropped into your shoes if you do.

Childish? Of course: very much so. Then why do it? Some would say letting off steam because you're so keyed up. But I don't *feel* keyed up or anything like it. And I don't think the rest are either. And yet we continue with these pranks. It's almost a religion. Maybe it's the only religion most of us have: I don't ever go to church services and I don't know of many who do, other than those who are Catholics.

**27 June 1984**

A rumour had been persisting here all month that ops over France, whether by night or by day, were each to count only as one third of an op. Which would mean that we had but one full op (Gelsenkirchen) to our credit, the 12 French efforts counting as four only. So we'd have five recorded and, if they were all to be over France, another 75 to do. Christ, another 75! A sentence of death, that's what it would be: you're absolutely bound to buy it with another 75 ahead of you, no matter where over.

The rumour modified itself recently. But only slightly – a French op was to count as half a German one. Still a sentence, by our reckoning.

Then today it was scotched. Orally, by a senior officer, but scotched all the same. Evidently there had been a goodly measure of truth behind this rumour: the intention definitely had been to give less credit for sorties over France, Belgium, etc. But, we were led to believe, two events had made the originators of this proposal change their minds. One was a daylight over France where predicted accurate flak shot down a surprising number of Lancs: the other was a night attack on a French railway goods-yard when the night fighters, aided by a clear, cloudless night, got into the bomber stream just over the French coast, stayed in it all the way to the target and still remained in it all the way back to the coast: in doing so they wreaked much havoc. (No aircraft from here in either of these raids.)

Yes, that was the end of *that* nonsense. Much to the relief of us all. So off to Vaires at 00:35, tomorrow morning, 28 June, knowing it'll count as a full one. It'll be our 13th . . .

**Later**

Not sleeping at all well these days (or in some cases, these nights).

Over the course of the first two or three ops I'd get into my bed, lie there tossing and turning, waiting for the sleep which seldom, if ever, came. Then, funnily enough, with those few under my belt, I could crawl in between the sheets and in a few minutes be sound asleep.

Suppose it's because I've now got over a third of the tour in and my subconscious is reflecting that you've made it so far, but remember that the guy with the great big chopper over his shoulder reckons he still has 18 chances to get you on to his books. Tiring, but I'm dead against taking any sleeping pills. Smoking rather heavily, I'm afraid, and that's drugs enough.

| | |
|---|---|
| *Op. No. 13* | *28 June 1944* |
| *Target* | Goods-yards at VAIRES (PARIS) |
| *A/C 'V'* | *Load* 18 x 500lbs. |
| *Take off* | 00:35 hrs. *Duration* 4:45 hrs. |
| *Height* | 13,000ft. |
| *Flak* | Nil |
| *E/A* | None sighted |
| *S/Ls* | Practically nil |

Good concentrated bombing. One a/c – P/O Guilfoyle, captain – missing from our station.

Boring, this effort. Funny, but before we took off, there was everybody saying well, it's our thirteenth, let's hope it's not the unlucky one; why can't we call it number 12A? Almost jittery simply because of that '13'. Then during it no flak, no night-fighters and just the odd searchlight. We had a feeling of anti-climax, I suppose.

Yet, Guilfoyle from here missing. Couldn't have been flak so practically the only conclusion can be that he must have strayed out of the stream and that, although we didn't sight any night-fighters, they were around somewhere – maybe not in the vicinity of Paris, but perhaps spaced out along the stream. Hope that he and his crew are in the bag.

One thing of beauty: dawn breaking as we crossed back over the French coast. Am not capable of describing the colours except to write that they were magnificent. A feeling of serenity flying there at 13,000ft. (gradually dropping height once clear of the coast) with another Lanc or two for company and there is this wonderfully, beautiful dawn ahead of us. Almost welcoming, it seemed.

A less attractive welcome as we dropped down through the cloud to find it bucketing down over Lincolnshire . . .

Cycled into Lincoln this late afternoon to go to the flicks. Just about to enter the cinema when found I'd forgotten my fags. None at the kiosk so walked around until I found a shop open. No, no Capstan, no Players and didn't I know there was a war on? As a favour sold me 20 Rhodian: they're smaller than Capstan but bigger than Woodbines. They cost 1/3d for 20 (either plain or corktips) and, as the name implies, are made of Rhodesian tobacco. Don't really fancy them, but better than nothing and keep me going until I get back to Wickenby where there's *never* a shortage of fags: in fact, some of the lads who're pally with civvies buy the odd packet for them there. Film was 'Yankee Doodle Dandy'; enjoyed Cagney's hoofing. The projectionist must have been a Miller fan because during the interval, and on the odd time in between, he played nothing but.

On coming outside, smell of fish and chips. Followed my nose until it led me to 'Frying Tonight' sign. A queue outside and in it just ahead of me Sergeants Norman and Dunn. Said I was feeling generous and would stand my hand! The guy doing the frying asked whether I wanted haddock suppers at a tanner each or hake at 5d. I said haddock. Funny, but the English – at least the English in these parts – eat all kinds of peculiar fish (such as hake) at which even a Scots cat would turn up its nose; and probably arch its back for good measure.

Said to Norman and Dunn I'd buy them a pint, but they explained that they were pushed to catch the last 'bus back to Wickenby so maybe some other time. So got on the Raleigh to cycle back. Didn't get very far though because the level crossing gates across the street opened to allow a fussy little engine to do some shunting. Back and forth it went, seemingly in no hurry and ignoring the two cars (and the cyclist!) it was holding up. Not that it worried me – I like engines.

Started raining on way back and regretted not taking raincoat. Got soaked and dismounted at a pub. Was dark by now and I don't know what it was called. Bloke in shirt sleeves behind bar put down his *Daily Mirror* when I asked for a large whisky and informed me I couldn't even have a *small* one: he hadn't had any whisky for a month. No gin either: in fact, he had no spirits of any kind. He didn't ask if I knew there was a war on, but his manner suggested the question. I got a pint of mild: give him his due, it was an excellent pint.

No difficulty with my Form 1250 at the Guard Room this time: I had remembered to transfer it from the one jacket to the other before leaving. So didn't have to end up inside to await the inevitable encounter with an irate Duty Officer. Suppose if it had been the same one as last time, instead of conveying to him my pleasure over George Shearing, I could have expressed my enjoyment of Cagney's hoofing . . .

Went directly to the Mess and sunk a large whisky, which helped dispel the chill feeling I had (on no account must I catch a cold and have to call off operational flying; or rather, be taken off it. Think of the crew having to fly with a spare bomb aimer, if available. Worse still, think of *me* having to catch up later, when they've done their 30, by doing my last ones with an inexperienced, and therefore chop-prone, crew).

Then into a hot bath. Reflect in it how easy I really have things compared, for example, to brown jobs maybe wet, dirty, sleeping when and where they can and in many cases in danger virtually all the time not just for a comparatively short, sharp spell such as I am. No, nothing to complain about.

Finally off to my pit with a good night's sleep in mind. But that just wouldn't come. Tossed and turned so much that I gave up trying and started reading.

**29 June 1944**

A spare hour or two before reporting for 'bus out to bay so decide to cycle round the perimeter track. All so peaceful, the Lancs lying noiselessly in their bays which are deserted save for the occasional fitter or wireless mechanic making some final check. Every Lanc has already been bombed-up and has been reported as fully serviceable. All that remains now is for the petrol bowsers to make their rounds and that's that. Apart from the crews, that is.

Yes, a peaceful sight. Set in the equally peaceful English countryside. Can hardly equate such peace with the fact that, before a couple of hours have gone, each of the four engines of each of those machines will snarl into angry life and will haul into the air seven men whose sole purpose is to convey a quantity of high explosive to a specific target and there to drop it.

Also can hardly equate the fenced-off, barbed wire area at the southern end of the airfield. 'Keep Out' signs, skull and crossbones, etc. That's where the mustard gas canisters are kept. Didn't quite believe that when first told, but it seems to be quite true. Only reason Hitler hasn't used gas is that he knows *we* have it. And that we'd use it. The one thing that keeps the bully boy off is the knowledge that he'll get more than he can hand out. They never learned that after 1919; peace-pledge unions, disarmament, all sorts of woolly-minded theories. Don't think we'll have these dafties after this war, though; no-one in his right mind can fail to see what happens to a country which can't defend itself against an aggressor.

| | |
|---|---|
| *Op. No. 14* | *29 June 1944* |
| *Target* | Robot-plane site at SIRRACOURT |
| *A/C 'V'* | *Load* 11 x 1,000lbs.<br>4 x 500lbs. |
| *Take off* | 12:10 hrs. *Duration* 3:45 hrs. |
| *Height* | 13,000ft. |
| *E/A* | Nil |
| *Flak* | Light, but what there was proved exceedingly accurate . . . heard the explosions of it all around the a/c and several bursts very very close to us, the shrapnel rattling all over the a/c; sounded rather like gigantic hailstones. Actually hit on the bombing run – on the port outer engine especially. Later counted ten very large flak holes and a number of smaller ones. Bombing seemed scattered for some reason or another – probably all that accurate flak, because, no doubt about it, when you're on your run-in and trying to get a really good sighting, flak bursting all around you is somewhat distracting. One a/c (P/O Underwood) missing from Wickenby. When I note some crew is missing I always live in hope that, later, we'll receive word that they're POW. But, sadly, you don't often receive such news and then you know they've had it |

Discovered one interesting item at interrogation. Which is that many bomb aimers, when on the run-in, lie on top of their steel helmet in such a way as to protect their testicles. Must say I hadn't thought of that. Somewhat uncomfortable I would have thought (but maybe not as uncomfortable as having your wedding tackle shot off!) Anyway, I'll take my chance of ending the tour speaking in a high falsetto voice. And in any case, I've lost my steel helmet; don't know where on earth it could have gone: it's not the kind of thing anybody's going to whip. Some day, I suppose, I'll be asked to account for it and, in its absence, will have to fork up something like a quid. (If the things cost *that* much to produce, which I doubt.)

That was yet another daylight one: our fourth. Still don't like daylights. Still feel naked and exposed stooging around over France with the sun shining and being very visible for miles around. Oh, I know there's lots of fighter cover, but, nevertheless, give me the dark every time. With this longing for the blackness of the night, am beginning to feel like old Dracula . . .

**29 June 1944**
Received a supplementary allocation of clothing coupons last week. Don't know on what this is based: presumably somebody at Air Ministry, on contemplating the date of your commission, decides that by this time you need a new uniform, or fresh shirts, underwear, socks, shoes, etc. Anyway, decided to go to Lincoln to get myself a new shirt. These coupons are strictly for military clothing and are not to be used for civilian attire. However, there is sometimes a way round this – if the establishment concerned sells military *and* civilian clothing! The department store I went to covers both. So, after buying a couple of shirts and handing over the necessary coupons, I glanced down at the remaining coupons and said I'd like to buy something for my fiancée. There was nobody else around and the assistant, after a slight hesitancy, asked what I had in mind. I replied I'd like a couple of pairs of stockings. She produced two pairs at 2/11d each, but they didn't look very clever. However, on my prompting she went away and returned with what seemed to be a couple of much better pairs. 'I'm afraid they're 4/11d per pair,' she apologised. I said OK. She said three coupons for them. Next a suspender belt at, I think, a couple of coupons and 5/11d. She seemed quite co-operative, especially as nobody else came in, that I went mad and forked up just over four quid and eight coupons for an unlined jacket (hope it fits Ann). Which left only two coupons. I gave them to the assistant for herself. She seemed quite pleased. Felt like trying to date her – she really was very attractive – but since I became engaged to Ann I'm behaving myself. Which, at times, is a bit difficult.

**30 June 1944**
An Anson landed at Wickenby yesterday and the pilot came into the Mess for lunch. Recognised his face immediately, but couldn't quite place it. Turned out to be an ex-regular NCO which whom I had trained as a pilot in Phoenix, Arizona, in 1942. Name of Kelly. Actually, we'd met earlier, in the previous year, when a bunch of ground staff, including myself, who were awaiting air crew training were summoned to an Air-Crew Receiving Centre (nicknamed 'Arsy-arsy') at Regent's Park, London. We were quartered in luxury flats, only they'd moved the luxury part before we got there. And we ate at the London Zoo nearby. We didn't enjoy the food all that much but I think the animals enjoyed watching us toying with it. Thereafter I'd moved with Kelly to No. 12 Initial Training Wing at St. Andrews (me at St. Andrews and I didn't know what a 'birdie' was unless it flew out of a tree and dropped one on me!) After that, Heaton Park, Manchester, then off on a transport to Canada before travelling south to Arizona.

I'd knocked around with him in Phoenix and, on the strength of that, asked for a flip in his Anson. He cleared this easily enough, merely telling Control he wanted to air test the kite. A more modern version of the ones we'd flown in Canada. There, as passenger, you had to wind up the undercart by hand which was a long, and tiring, job: this one retracted without any physical effort on anybody's part.

Once airborne, he handed over to me and we stooged quite happily over Lincoln and the surrounding country.

I feel sorry for Kelly. He's been landed in Flying Training Command and is desperate to get on ops. But it seems that once in FTC you're there for ever. A pity.

We promised to keep in touch. Neither meant it.

**30 June 1944**

When commissioned we were informed we were required to wear the VR badge. These are small (about ½″ high) chrome badges which are worn on both lapels of your Number One uniform and on the epaulettes. (Airmen wear cloth ones on their sleeves.) This requirement was to distinguish us from Regular officers: who, no doubt, considered themselves a different breed from those of us in the Volunteer Reserve. Never worried us; we rather liked them.

But recently an Order was issued instructing all Volunteer Reserve officers to remove their VR badges. Not much of a problem as regards those on the epaulettes, but to remove them from the lapels of your Number One left two unsightly holes which no amount of expert needlework could disguise. So most of us left them in our Number One jacket.

The Order has been repeated so I expect we'll have to conform. But what's the reason behind it? Could it be that the Regulars are now finding that some of the ignorant civilian populace have been drawing attention to us with our badges signifying that we are volunteers and inferring that any officer not wearing same must therefore be a conscript? Surely not. But there must be some reason or another.

| *Op. No. 15* | *30 June – 1 July 1944* |
|---|---|
| *Target* | Marshalling yards at VIERZON (South of Orleans) |
| *A/C 'V'* | *Load* 11 x 1,000lbs.<br>4 x 500lbs. |
| *Take off* | 21:30 hrs. *Duration* 5:30 hrs. |
| *Height* | 7,000ft. |
| *S/Ls* | One! |
| *Flak* | About four guns in all. And they seemed quite half-hearted at that, the flak being very light |
| *E/A* | Very active indeed by the number of fighter flares dropped on and around us. Fighters followed us all the way back to the French coast – still dropping flares. Saw a number of Lancs shot down so the Luftwaffe must have got right into the stream (or the Lancs strayed from it). Graceful and horrendous sight watching a burning Lanc slowly spiralling earthwards |

Found out later that this was the only raid laid on last night; which accounts for the numerous night fighters about; they'd be vectored on to our path from all over the place. 100 a/c took part. 15 shot down. 2 missing from 626 Squadron and 2 from 12 Squadron – P/Os Pollard and Honour, the latter being on his twenty-eighth op. Hard luck to do so many and then buy it with just another couple to go. God! Just two to go and you get it.

Marshalling yards exceedingly thoroughly bombed. Saw many explosions, all of which were very colourful. Makes me wonder if they'll ever be able to get these yards into operation again.

Not an easy one, like so many of these French efforts. And to think that a bright boy somewhere tried to have them count as only one-third of an op! You can't shrug off a loss of 15 Lancs, really.

Half-way through the tour now. I had never thought we'd make that half-way mark. But then, we've been lucky, despite what I've said above, that so many of our French ones have been so easy.

Was glad to get back on nights again. True, it was only dusk when we hit the French coast, but the darkness rose up at us as we flew south and, in a surprisingly short space of time, completely enfolded us. Felt much more comfortable then: much safer. Yes, I'll take the nights any time. Spoken to quite a few of the chaps about this and find, to my surprise, that one or two prefer the daylights. Say they'd rather see what's coming to them. Me, I don't want to see!

Note that we have done exactly 65 hours and 50 minutes of operational flying.

**1 July 1944**

Included in a letter from home today a paragraph of praise from my stepfather for the wool/silk underwear I'd sent him. We had been issued with two pairs: the vest had long sleeves and the underpants went as far as one's ankles. Wore a set just once and nearly sweated to death. (Would be just the job if trying to lose weight.) Anyway, my stepfather thinks they're terrific quality and absolutely spot-on.

But everything I've been issued with by the RAF has been of very high quality. Am even using still some of the gear issued to me when I reported to the Recruit Centre at Blackpool in mid-1940, particularly shaving brush, hair brushes and shoe brushes. (Quite enjoyed the square-bashing at Blackpool. Conducted on the Promenade and always surrounded by flocks of holiday-makers who obviously enjoyed the free entertainment. Not so an old dear when the Drill Corporal, quite justifiably in his professional opinion, called a recruit alongside me: 'a dozy bastard' – she rushed out and hit him on the head with her umbrella. Painful: for us, trying not to laugh.)

The only times I found this high quality superseded was when in America and Canada. In Phoenix, as cadets, we were issued with US Army shirts (6) and US Army slacks (3 pairs). Cut and quality both outstanding. Also leather shoes (3 pairs) which were comfort itself the second you slipped them on. Then up in Canada the RCAF decided we could do with re-equipping and gave us uniforms so immaculate one would have thought they were tailored to fit. All of which endeared the RCAF to us.

The RCAF endeared itself even more when I was instructing in 1942 back at No. 7 Bombing and Gunnery School at Paulson, Manitoba (where earlier I'd been as a cadet). The RCAF, deciding that it was unfair to pay their own people a certain rate and us a far lower one, decreed that ours would be upped to match theirs. So my daily rate of pay jumped from about three bucks to seven. Just like that. Yes, certainly endearing. Heard later that the additional funds for this increase to RAF personnel were provided by the Canadian Government. Very generous, I'd say.

**1 July 1944**

Understand some of the air-crew NCOs have it a bit rough in the Sergeants' Mess from time to time. This, because so many of the 'old sweats' are Regulars who had to wait years before attaining the rank of Leading Aircraftman, more years to Corporal, even more before making Sergeant: accordingly, they view with disfavour air-crew Sergeants who have achieved the rank after perhaps less than a year in the Service. They sometimes forget that they are safe as houses here at Wickenby while the air-crew Sergeants for the most part don't live long enough to really 'enjoy' (if that is the word) their NCO status. But, thankfully, all the non-flying NCOs don't act like this.

On the subject of non-flying NCOs, the Sergeant rigger who services our Lanc came out with a real beauty after our raid on the robot-plane site at Sirracourt. I had counted four large flak holes in 'V' for Victor. Evidently he had counted a lot more in parts of the aircraft I hadn't even looked at because he said to Vernon: 'What the bloody hell have you been doing to my aeroplane?'

What had *Vernon* been doing to *his* aeroplane! Give Vernon his due, he rose to the occasion and promised to try to be more careful next time . . .

That Sergeant had the holes patched up in no time at all.

The attitude towards us of the ground staff who service the Lanc is worth noting. For even one of them to salute either Vernon, Horsfall or myself would have been unthinkable. And regarding the word 'Sir', as far as we are concerned that has disappeared completely from their vocabulary. They address Vernon as 'skipper', Horsfall as 'Ted' (how they know his Christian name defeats me), myself as the inescapable 'Jock', and the Sergeants by a variety of names ranging from their Christian ones to 'bugger-lugs' and 'piss-quick'.

They are all good types.

On your return you need only one of them to marshal you from the perimeter track into your bay: but invariably on our return we find most, if not all, of them hanging around in the bay, even when they could be in their billets. They give the impression that their only interest is the state of the aircraft.

**1 July 1944 (Entered later)**

Relations with one member of the ground-staff are now slightly strained albeit only temporary, I hope. In preparation for the attack on Vierzon Dunn had climbed into the Lanc to go to inspect his wireless equipment. On nearing his compartment, he observed a body bending over it with behind high in the air. Gently he stroked it, at the same time making endearing noises. Imagine his surprise when a WAAF straightened herself up and belted him a right hefty one across the cheek!

| | |
|---|---|
| *Op. No. 16* | *2 July 1944* |
| *Target* | Robot-plane supply site at DOMLEGER |
| *A/C 'V'* | *Load* 11 x 1,000lbs.<br>4 x 500lbs. |
| *Take off* | 12:30 hrs. *Duration* 3:15 hrs. |
| *Height* | 13,500ft. |
| *Flak* | Very light: only about 3 or 4 heavy guns around the site. No bursts near us |
| *E/A* | None around |

Another of these robot-plane sites. Those things must be doing an awful lot of damage judging by the number of times we have to bomb them. Sky cloudy, but site well plastered. And, of course, so much fighter cover we're in danger of being crowded out of the bloody sky. What a beauty that Spitfire is! She's so graceful. (But then, so is our Lanc.) Yet, despite the beauty of the Spit and the fact that they're swarming all around us, I *still* don't like these daylight efforts. And never will.

I announce, after I've dropped my bombs, closed the bomb-doors and had a quick look up the bay for hang-ups, that today is my 23rd birthday.

To which Horsfall retorts that surely I don't expect a present from him? I reply that from a Yorkshireman you don't expect anything other than brass neck.

Vernon cuts into this cross-talk by mildly observing that he wouldn't like to bet on my making my 24th, that we are having it easy on those French robot-plane sites etc., but that when they get back to putting us on to devastating the Third Reich my chances of making that 24th will be reduced by, he reckons, about 75 per cent. He doesn't mention that that pessimistic percentage applies to him also.

All this cross-talk is very unprofessional. Shouldn't be indulging in it. You're not 100 per cent on the ball for eventualities when you're yacking away over the intercom. Sign of over-confidence: you could pay for it.

It's a very pleasant English summer's evening and we're just over half-way through our operational tour, so maybe I should put something down in this Diary about the other members of the crew.

*Pilot:* F/O Vernon. An American, from Maine or thereabouts. A very good pilot. When we go into the bombing run he responds rather immaculately to my 'left-lefts', 'right a wee bit' and so on. Then holds her as steady as a rock. Does not comment much on the proceedings except to observe, on occasions when the flak is intense: 'Christ, look at all that shit coming our way'.

*Navigator:* Sgt. Norman. Comes from somewhere about the Midlands, I think. Right from the beginning he maintained his firm intention of remaining behind the curtains in his little navigation compartment getting on with his work, that he didn't want to see anything that was, in his own words: 'going to blast up my arse.' Was persuaded to put out his navigator's light and open his curtains while we were over Gelsenkirchen. He saw the wall of flak, shouted: 'Fuck me!' and has not emerged since: not during a raid that is. Says wild horses wouldn't drag him out again during an op and ignores questions as to how you could get any horse into a Lanc, far less a wild one.

*Engineer:* Sgt. Griggs. Pleasant: maybe about a couple of years younger than we are. Seems over-awed a bit by Vernon, Horsfall and myself: and, sometimes, quite shocked.

*Mid-upper Gunner:* P/O Horsfall. Being a regular who volunteered for air crew, he's perhaps a couple of years older than we are. A Yorkshire man with rather an abrasive personality. A health fiend – rugger and all sorts of dreadful exercises.

*Wireless Operator:* Sgt. Dunn. He has nothing to do for most of the time except to maintain a listening watch. During our operational flights he sits in his blacked out compartment and reads Westerns. Someone asks him if he can't read anything better than these wretched Westerns: he says he's tried murder mysteries, but that they're not exciting enough. Imagine – all that going on and he sits there reading Westerns!

*Rear Gunner:* Sgt. Cartwright. A quiet, dependable chap who, for the most part, keeps himself to himself.

Generally, we are not a closely-knit crew: we do not, for instance, go out on pub crawls together. Most of the other crews seem to do this, but not us. In fact, I think the only thing we all have in common is the constant use of the copulative adjective, even Sgt. Griggs using the word now and then. I think nearly all of us now find it hard to string a sentence together without lacing it with the adjective, often more than just once. But we fly well together and that is the main thing.

**Later**

Those robot-bombs which are launched from the installations we've been pranging must be taking up a considerable amount of the

German war effort. Not so sure they wouldn't have been wiser to expend material and energy on building better bombers with which to attack us rather than these things. When a Luftwaffe bomber is shot down German resources are reduced by that much, but if it is not it lives to fly, and bomb, again. These bombs, on the other hand, once they're launched that's the end of the matter: also, the Germans don't know whether they've hit the target or have been shot down over the sea.

On that subject, the Hawker Tempest, with its high speed, seems to have come into its own. It can catch up with the robot-bomb, which, of course, cannot take any form of evasive action, and fly quite close to it before opening up (with, naturally, no fear of retaliation!) Hits anywhere on the robot and that's it killed. Nasty things, all the same: wouldn't like to be on the deck, hear one of those efforts drone overhead then, worst of all, hear its engine cut (which means it's about to plunge down).

**3 July 1944**

Had observed earlier on that there's always plenty to keep you occupied here at Wickenby when not flying. A further example of this today: informed Vernon and Horsfall that I was off to the Intelligence Reading Room and were they coming? On their both agreeing, Vernon commented that Horsfall was coming only because *Picture Post* this week had a pair of nice tits in it, laying himself open to Horsfall's retort that, if this were the case, Vernon had been bloody quick off the mark in grabbing a copy of it.

But *Picture Post* is only in the Reading Room as an extra: all sorts of journals and magazines there, both official and semi-official. Vernon buried himself in the exploits of Pilot Officer Prune exhorting certain flying characters to get their fingers out in future so as to avoid a series of inexcusable accidents: and, by his odd chuckle, obviously was content. Horsfall started examining in detail a large diagram, which had just been pinned up, of an installation of two Oerlikon 20mm cannon mounted in the fuselage of the ME110 night fighter and arranged to fire upwards and forwards at an angle of between ten and twenty degrees from the vertical. This was a newish installation which enabled night fighters to make attacks from below where the Lanc presented quite a large target, was nearly blind, and was almost unable to defend itself – from the rear turret or anywhere else. As I too examined it, he observed: 'And that's where we're going to be shot up the arse from if we're not careful.' I replied that if we were I'd blame him for not keeping a spot-on lookout, which I told him I was positive he hadn't been keeping before now.

Suppose he got his own back a short while later. I was examining a chart concerning German anti-aircraft defences and, when he came alongside me, pointed out that Flak was short for Fliegerabwehrkanonen (anti-aircraft guns) and that the German WAAFs who manned their operation rooms were called Luftwaffenhelferinen. He gave me a long, steady look and said: 'So effing hell what?'

After that, together we contemplated a photograph of Goering examining an ME110 with some special equipment for homing on to enemy bombers. (How such photographs arrive here in the UK defeats us, but come out of Germany they certainly do.) Horsfall informs me that he 'doesn't mind old Hermann' and I agree with him. Funny, but virtually nobody here at Wickenby, when the fat Reichsmarschall's name crops up in conversation, seems to have a bad word for him, despite what went on when we were at the receiving end of his Luftwaffe. The reason is not absolutely clear. Perhaps the firmly held belief that Goering, as Number 2 in the Nazi pecking order, has made it clear to all and sundry that shot down RAF bods are his, that they are under his personal protection, has something to do with it. Personally, I'm not so sure about this; conflicts with other stories we hear.

Just about finished there when in come two of our sergeants: they look about in not very interested fashion and settle for a combined examination of *Picture Post*. Eventually, they go off somewhere with Vernon and Horsfall for a game of Pontoon. I'm not invited: they know I don't go much on playing pontoon; according to Horsfall it's because I once lost a couple of bob at the game. In actual fact, I consider card games a waste of time: would much rather amuse myself in other ways. Like filling up this black notebook, for example. (Have already bought Mark II for the continuation: cost 8d – up tuppence over these three months or so.)

**4 July 1944**

Chatting today to a rigger working on our Lanc. Discovered he too had been with the RAF in Canada. Therefore assumed he was failed aircrew. Not so; he was sent out there, when the Empire Air Training Scheme first got under way, to work on the kites which were to fly from the new airfields being constructed.

His experiences there were in some respects rather similar to mine. As regards the birds, I mean. He too, made the mistake of informing one that he'd 'knock her up tomorrow evening', in complete ignorance of the difference in meaning of these words. Only, in his case, he was unwittingly giving her advance notice of the earlier stages of his proposed activities over that evening – with a bit of luck avoiding her reaching the latter physical state which the phrase covers. Warmed to his subject did this fitter, his work on the Lanc of secondary importance meantime. After an exhausting week in New Brunswick, he had decided that his major contribution to the war effort would be keeping the Canadian birds happy by, in his own words: 'shagging my way from East to West and ending up completely knackered.'

From what had now become a monologue on his part, it seemed that the 'knackered' stage was never reached. Not by any decrease in his spirit or intention, or, indeed, capability, but by the arrival of the aircrew cadets from the UK. The cadets, usually better-educated than the ground crews, were also more polished, more sophisticated: and they had much better lines to shoot at the girls. Also, while their intentions towards them in no whit differed from those of the ground crews ('the buggers were all after the same thing,' grimaced the fitter) they didn't rush headlong into the proceedings. As a result, the first comers found themselves edged out and in many cases soon became dateless: a most unhappy state of affairs for them, who, until then, had reigned supreme.

At this, I started making sympathetic noises. They were unnecessary because his grimace had now changed itself into a grin. He said that the penny had well and truly dropped when they were at an airfield in Western Ontario. The next one to be constructed was in Eastern Manitoba: when they arrived there and had established relations with the local girls (which didn't take him long, he boasted) they informed them that, shortly, other RAF bods would be appearing. These bods would be wearing little white flashes in their caps – which all aircrew cadets did. They *had* to wear them, the girls were told, because they had VD, or had had it and were in the process of being cured.

At this stage my fitter friend could hardly continue for laughing. The cadets had wondered why they were getting the cold shoulder from the girls: and by the time they, or at least some of them, had managed to convince females that the white flash meant aircrew cadet and nothing else, the ground crews had moved West to new fields (in more ways than one).

I said all very interesting, but I had to get down to the Armoury now. To my surprise he cocked me up one. On reflection, considering the subject matter concerned, that, perhaps, is not the best of phrases to describe a salute. But once anything is entered, I don't like altering. I suppose it's pretty apt anyway . . .

**Later**

About a week later, when I went out to the bay to check over some items on the Lanc, this fitter was again working on it. Seemed anxious to hand me another instalment of his sexual activities across the length and breadth of Canada. I said I was pushed for time, otherwise I'd be delighted to hear them. This time no salute when I left.

| | |
|---|---|
| *Op. No. 17* | *4 July 1944* |
| *Target* | Marshalling yards at ORLEANS |
| *A/C 'B'* | *Load* 11 x 1,000lbs.<br>4 x 500lbs. |
| *Take off* | 22:25 hrs. *Duration* 6:30 hrs. |
| *Height* | 8,000ft. |
| *Flak* | Very light |
| *E/A* | Plenty of night fighters around: saw what looked like a ME109 from the front turret, but he did not attack. One a/c (F/S Turner) lost from Wickenby |

Yet another one on French marshalling yards. Wonder who mans these trains which use them. Is it Frenchmen? Doubt it: maybe the Germans have their own engine drivers and firemen for what must be very dangerous jobs. Also wonder why on this particular night so many fighters around: could be that all this bombing of marshalling yards is having such an effect on troop and munition movements that the Luftwaffe is transferring night fighters from Germany to France in an attempt to counter it.

We have another brand new a/c, 'B' for Baker. Not that there was anything wrong with 'V' for Victor: this is the first Lanc to come to our Squadron equipped with a new radar gadget called $H_2S$ which enables you to 'see' through cloud, and Winco Nelson told us he wanted an experienced crew for it. To which we replied that flattery would get him nowhere. Think this $H_2S$ is going to be OK: after mucking about with it I started getting pin-points through the clouds. They weren't all that clear, though: my lack of expertise on the gadget, I'd say – I'll need to play about with it a lot more to obtain maximum effect: a training exercise for this purpose alone would be a good idea.

| | |
|---|---|
| *Op. No. 18* | *5-6 July 1944* |
| *Target* | Marshalling yards at DIJON |
| *A/C 'B'* | *Load* 8 x 1,000lbs.<br>3 x 500lbs. |
| *Take off* | 21:10 hrs. *Duration* 8.55 hrs. |
| *Height* | 7,000ft. |
| *Flak* | Very light |
| *S/Ls* | Nil |
| *E/A* | None sighted |

Bright moonlight. Which means no cloud cover which makes happy hunting for night fighters. Really surprising that no contacts were made. So different to last night when there were so many around.

No a/c missing from Wickenby: indeed, no a/c at all missing from this op.

With all this concentrated bombing of marshalling yards virtually no German armour, no German troops, must be getting through to the front. At least, not by rail. We are all becoming somewhat bored.

Noticed, at Interrogation, Winco Nelson conducting three civvies around. Probably some big-wigs from Air Ministry or Ministers, maybe even MPs. After contemplating the Order of Battle and listening to what the Winco had to say concerning it, they started questioning some of the crews. One of them started to edge towards us but the Winco very craftily edged him away from us again. I think he was going to take no chances. He's well aware of Vernon's stock reply when asked by any WAAF officer who hasn't de-briefed us before to report on any damage: it is 'only to my wedding tackle'. (One innocent lass actually wrote this down on her form before somebody's guffaw made her reach for her eraser!) Think Winco maybe was afraid one of his distinguished visitors would put this question and receive this answer. Also perhaps, that other questions put to us might receive answers which would reflect no credit on No. 12 Squadron and which could result in a rather nasty letter from higher authority.

His fears really were groundless. I think.

**6 July 1944**

Just leaving the Mess after lunch when buttonholed by Winco Nelson. Asked how things were, and so on. Then informed me that there was to be some kind of celebration in the NCOs' Mess tonight, that it was customary for a couple of officers to look in for a brief spell in the earlier part of the evening, that he was going and would I care to join him? Winco Nelson is the kind of man who, if you'd thanked him but said you had a heavy date in Lincoln, would never dream of letting you cancel it. He's also the kind of man for whom I would have insisted on cancelling such a date had I had one. So I thanked him and said I'd be delighted.

We turned up at the NCOs' Mess at eight o'clock to be greeted by the SWO who immediately conducted us to the bar. No question of Winco or me paying – on the house. With Winco chatting away with the SWO I was able to look around. Not many signs of celebrations so far. Some sergeants sitting reading, some playing snooker, four WAAFs playing cards. Also Dunn and Griggs playing shove-ha'penny. Dunn saw me and gave a wave after which they concluded their game and came across to the bar. I refused their offer of a drink, but they insisted. Yacked away with them for a while but could not, of course, reciprocate. Then they drifted off. Nursed that second pint carefully keeping it in measure with Winco Nelson's. Because, when the Winco leaves, *you* leave. Had just started an interesting chat with a F/S bomb aimer when a WAAF sergeant put a record on the radiogram (another immaculate HMV effort like our own). It was Basie's 'One O'Clock Jump' and it was played at full boost. Next several couples were jitterbugging. I saw Winco Nelson finish the remains of his pint and make the slightest of movements towards the door. I sank what was left of mine, followed Winco in thanking the SWO for his hospitality and left with the Winco.

Outside, Winco Nelson, saying that his thirst had only been slightly slaked, took me back to our own Mess and bought me another pint refusing to have one on me.

Would really have liked to have stayed on longer at the NCOs' Mess. As well as that interesting chat, it looked as if things were hotting up. Which is precisely why the officers have to leave. Protocol, in effect: the officers go as guests of the SWO who remains with them all the time, stay for just a couple of drinks, then leave. To stay longer would incur the possibility of some NCO who had perhaps become rather tanked up saying, or even doing, something which would be very prejudicial to good discipline. Then even with that jitterbugging: had I been silly enough to remain longer, in the unlikely event of a WAAF inviting me to dance, I would have had to decline. Perhaps giving grave offence which, depending on how much she'd drunk, she might well have expressed.

Yes, would have had to decline. Not because of difference of rank: because on the dance floor I'm about as graceful as an elephant.

| | |
|---|---|
| *Op. No. 19* | *7 July 1944* |
| *Target* | Armour and troop concentrations at CAEN |
| *A/C 'B'* | *Load* 11 x 1,000lbs.<br>4 x 500lbs. |
| *Take off* | 19:15 hrs. *Duration* 3:50 hrs. |
| *Height* | 7,000ft. |
| *Flak* | On the light side over target, but heavier around the coast |
| *E/A* | Nil |

Another daylight op. We were told that very accurate bombing was essential – 'bring the things back if you can't be sure of your aiming point'. This because we were bombing only 1½ miles ahead of our troops (Canadians, evidently). My sighting was not right so I didn't press the tit. I told Vernon to go round a second time. God, the language which came over that intercom! Interspersed with references not only to my complete inadequacy as a bomb aimer, but also to my parentage. Can't exactly blame them – there we were, the only Lanc left over Caen and what flak there was beginning to concentrate on us. But there was no way I was going to drop 13,000lbs of high explosive when there was the slightest possibility of the dreadful stuff killing or wounding our own troops: would have taken the load back to Wickenby first. However, I got a perfect sighting on that second run (despite what was still being said over the intercom) and placed my bombs exactly where I wanted them.

Despite that second time round, on the way back we caught up with the stragglers ('B' for Baker being brand new and with that extra few knots more than most). Flying almost level with another Lanc, who was limping. Just crossing the French coast when up came quite a scything of flak. It got him (not, by the Grace of God, us). He started diving straight down. We counted four parachutes opening, prayed for more but to no avail. The Lanc struck the water, burst into a terrific sheet of flame. We all fell silent until over base, everybody thinking of the three men inside.

**9 July 1944**

Yesterday, decided to forego writing. Not that I'm becoming tired of it; really, I think, because I'm turning into a sort of compulsive scribbler. Can't wait to write up the latest op, or anything of interest (to me) which happens here, sometimes even hurrying my meals in order to do so. The thing has, in a way, taken me over. I bought the notebook with the intention solely of entering in it brief details of each op just after it had taken place and nothing else. Now all sorts of items connected with Wickenby but not really in any way connected with operational flying have found – and no doubt will continue to find – their way into it. In fact, when I flick back over the pages the non-operational stuff seems to have swamped what set out to be a diary of thirty (Christ, I hope it *is* thirty!) operational flights over Germany and Occupied Europe with, perhaps, a few pages covering events on first arriving at 12 Squadron. So yesterday it remained untouched.

Instead, in the evening, there being nothing doing, I lay on top of my bed and turned on the radio. A four valve Ferranti bought second hand (naturally, with no radios being produced nowadays) in Lincoln for £5. Same model that my stepfather bought in 1938 for £4, but no doubt he had got a discount on it, having a pal in the trade, so probably a fiver was fair enough. Twiddled the dial and listened to some station featuring Miller: played 'Perfidia' (with those immaculate Modernaires) then Ray Eberle singing 'At Last'. Wished I'd tuned in earlier because those two were the end of the programme. Radio Athlone or thereabouts.

More twiddling and Lord Haw-Haw. Listened to him telling me what a swine I was dropping bombs on innocent civilians. Jesus wept! That bloody nation was all behind Hitler when he was winning: there's nothing innocent about them. No talk about swine when bombing Coventry: or when on that dreadful raid on Clydebank. They're getting what they deserve. And I'm glad to be one of those dishing it out to them. Heavens, get me an orange box and I'll get on to it!

But that bugger Joyce. They say they'll hang him after the war. And he deserves it: for that nasal, grating voice of his as much as for what he says. Which they will. If they ever catch him.

Reflect that if somebody comes in while I'm listening to Haw-Haw all that will happen is that the radio will get a two-fingered salute: no hasty effort will be made to turn it off. A different reaction if some Luftwaffe type discovered lying on his bed listening to the BBC. Also reflect that many of those Luftwaffe aircrew must be characters not unlike ourselves with, perhaps, similar education, similar standards and yet they're fighting for a cruel, evil dictator maintained in power by what is no more than a bunch of gangsters. Yet I reckon that, to them, they're fighting for their country. And, in any case, supposing our own regime was one I detested, I think I would be doing the same.

Was tempted last night, after listening to Joyce and reflecting on him and the Luftwaffe boys, to get up and fill another page or two of this effort. But resisted. Got up certainly. But only to go for a pint. Sandy Mansfield was at the bar looking bored. He bought me one; I bought him one. Then a couple or so times round again. When arrived back at my room didn't feel the least bit like writing.

**10 July 1944**
Interesting to read a report in today's papers about bulldozers clearing devastated Caen: these have had to be called in to plough the roads because the damage is so great that our tanks cannot advance. Evidently Caen is all devastation, there being a strip of land around the northern suburbs, about a quarter mile wide, which is nothing but a mass of rubble.

Was heartened, however, to read that the author of the report, in paying tribute to the careful aiming of the RAF, states that the thick belt of complete destructions starts right at the end of the city proper; and that, while the famous old Caen Cathedral has been damaged, it has not been destroyed; and that the two ancient abbeys are also still intact. Makes me glad I went round that second time on 7 July.

**15 July 1944**
That was quick – a sudden short leave. From afternoon of 10 July until today. Enough time to nip up to Edinburgh (hauled by 'Sir Nigel Gresley' looking a bit worse for wear). Became engaged to Ann. No question of marriage. Not yet: wait until I've got my tour over; maybe even wait until the end of the war. But that lass is for me. She's a secretary and her boss is T. F. Cameron, Divisional General Manager (Scottish Area) of the LNER. She gets free passes on the railway. Ah well, I got a warrant for my journey to Edinburgh and back . . .

On return here find we're stood down. Duff weather.

**16 July 1944**
Being stood-down 'they' usually have a job for you.

But this time it's not in the least an enjoyable one. Together with some F/O, whose name I forget, I form a Committee of Adjustment. This is an entirely ridiculous title for two of you who go through someone's personal effects.

When a Lanc doesn't make it back to Wickenby, the RAF wait a few days for the gen to reach them as to its fate. If the Lanc hasn't made it to some other airfield in the UK, then the crew are either dead or are POW. It is at this stage that the Committee of Adjustment are appointed at the Lanc's home station to deal with the effects of each of the lost aircrew – in my case a P/O navigator. This is the procedure. The two of you go to this P/O's room and sift through everything that's in his locker. The whole point of this exercise is that all he has is to be returned to his next-of-kin. And the exercise requires two of you so that, in the most unlikely event of that next-of-kin, on receiving these effects, claiming that some expensive item of his was not among them, the RAF can reply that two officers carefully examined all his effects and that that item simply was not there. And that they have signed accordingly.

You've got to be very careful. For instance, you check for FLs: you wouldn't return these to some fond mother who had never for a moment thought her son would indulge in that sort of thing. Same for pornographic photos. And the letters he retained, well, you had to read them to see what was in them and who they came from; after all, maybe there was a fiancée.

Yes, a careful assignment it was.

But this P/O was married. I'm not recording his name; despite all I say, what I'm writing now might well come into other people's hands and, if read, could cause extreme unhappiness. And there's enough of *that* around these days without my adding to it.

That's enough writing for today – I'm off to the Mess for a pint. Strong rumours of more leave for aircrew in a day or so. Hope it's true. Can continue about this P/O's effects after it. Surely, I can hardly get the chop in Edinburgh can I? Unless I get knocked down by a tram in Princes Street . . .

Rumours of more leave not true. So might as well finish what I was recording about this P/O's effects. (Christ, how this does ramble!)

The guy, as I've noted above, was married. Extremely handsome – looked like Errol Flynn. But as randy as hell (which kind of fits, I suppose – EF is supposed to be like that). Really, any attractive girl, whether civvy of WAAF, was a challenge to him: he went all out to shag her. He used to say that he was certain that he would buy it during the tour and that accordingly, even though married, he was going to 'do' every woman he could. Someone in the Mess once said: 'God, you'll shag yourself to death.' To which he retorted: 'Isn't that a better way than being shot down?' There is, of course, no answer to such a retort. According to what we discovered, he lived up to this. There were, for instance, enough FLs to kit out the entire Squadron. And he must have had immense charm to persuade girls to fall for him as they did. As for the letters, well, they all went into the fire. We checked and double checked that nothing which was returned to his wife would give her any impression other than that of a devoted and faithful husband.

PS *Added end July*. Learned he's in the bag. Ah, well, no nookie for him there.

But that was a Committee of Adjustment which ended up on a comparatively light note. Most don't. And one pilot admitted to me that it was the most upsetting job he'd ever been handed since coming here to Wickenby. He knew the bod concerned had been killed, because he had been right next to him over the target, had seen the other receive a direct hit from flak, seen it explode with nobody getting out. He found going through the dead chap's effects a numbing experience: felt there was something pathetic about the trivial items which the dead man had so obviously treasured and visualised the parents when these items where returned to them. He was almost unable to read the letters from his parents and found his eyes watering to read phrases like: 'May God protect you and return you safely to us': 'We pray for you every night.'

While nodding my understanding, I said that Winco Nelson had an even more disturbing task: he had to write to these parents (maybe he doesn't *have* to, but I understand that he does) and couch his letter in such a way as to try to give them some comfort, which I'd reckon is almost impossible. Then the Padre too had to write similarly: and not just now and then what with all these losses.

One thing I do know about these Committees of Adjustment: and that is that nobody on them would retain any item for himself no matter how trivial. Even if your uniform was on the scruffy side and the deceased's was brand new and a perfect fit you'd never think of switching. Would be ghoulish, that. Don't know what would happen if the parents wrote and said they didn't want his uniform back. Would probably be put up for sale in the Mess. But would they forward the proceeds of this sad sale to the parents? Doubt it; somehow or another it wouldn't seem right. Must find out about that sometime. Wonder if my parents would want my uniform back if I get the chop. What on earth would they do with it? Would, I think, be a constant, sad reminder to them that once I wore it.

**17 July 1944**

The Station cinema's a good refuge when not flying and at rather a loose end. Not very democratic, I'm afraid, in RAF cinemas the two back rows invariably being reserved for officers, the next three or four for NCOs and the remainder a free-for-all for airmen and WAAFs. Still, I suppose it's got to be that way; you couldn't have officers jostling with all and sundry for the best seats – not very conducive to good discipline.

One of the most enjoyable facets of the cinema here (and this applies more or less to all Station cinemas in the RAF) is the constant barrage of wisecracks from the audience should the film lend itself to them. It only needs someone on the screen to express surprise at a particular item and to ask what he, or she, should do with it. The advice, which never varies, is usually provided from all over the cinema, the WAAFs being prominent in their offering of it.

Such advice, however, varies. In one RAF cinema (at Dumfries, I think) they showed an ancient effort in which Hedy Lamarr debarked from a rowing boat at some remote island off some unspecified coast to be surrounded immediately by a mob of savages who, according to what passed for a plot, had never seen a white person before and were shrieking away in hostile gibberish. Undaunted, Hedy said: 'Take me to your leader.'

This provoked much merriment among the audience. More merriment when, from the front stalls, someone advised: 'Take her to the bloody Groupie' which, in turn, was followed by: 'Who'll have them down even before she knows it.' The Group Captain was not present at the screening, which was perhaps just as well.

Saw at Wickenby – for the second time – the film called: 'Thunderbirds' part of which had been shot at Falcon Field, Arizona, when I was there. Again glimpsed myself for a brief second or so. Was careful not to tell anybody I had such a big part in this film. It went down quite well with the audience only Reginald Denny, as an RAF officer, receiving any advice. Which was to 'get some in'. I don't think British actors who are staying in America for the duration of the war instead of returning here come in for much criticism from RAF types who, on the whole, feel that probably they're doing more for the war effort there than they could here. True, they're safe, and making a packet, but that's the luck of the game. Certainly, when Gracie Fields came to Falcon Field to sing for us neither I nor anybody else held it against here that she was in America and not back home. (Some didn't go much on her new husband – Monty somebody-or-another – but he seemed to me to be a pleasant enough person.) Gracie, of course, sang 'Sally'. Twice.

One film that went down well in the Station cinema here was: 'In Which We Serve'. No cracks at this one: it was watched, and listened to, in complete silence. About the only thing you could *almost* hear was the wave of sympathy for Richard Attenborough when he couldn't take any more.

| | |
|---|---|
| *Op. No. 20* | *18-19 July 1944* |
| *Target* | Synthetic oil refinery at GELSENKIRCHEN (RUHR) |
| *A/C 'B'* | *Load* 1 x 4,000lbs.<br>18 x 500lbs. |
| *Take off* | 22:50 hrs. *Duration* 4:40 hrs. |
| *Height* | 19,000ft. |
| *Flak* | Heavy |
| *S/Ls* | Very concentrated: so many cones that it was difficult to avoid flying through them. More S/Ls than have ever seen before. Some fighter flares. Saw a single-engined fighter in a dive. Three times tailed, but on each occasion we corkscrewed violently. According to Cartwright, one seemed to follow us down, then up, then down again before breaking off to look for easier game elsewhere. |

Got it again – that knot in the stomach: the instant when, at the bomb aimers' pre-briefing, the target was revealed as Gelsenkirchen. Suppose it was brought about by the recollection of our earlier raid on that city plus the acceptance that all the easy stuff over France was now finished and that this was the resumption of the big ones on Germany. Stayed with me during the main briefing right until we took off. Then, true to form, it disappeared. Must have a thing about this knot in the guts the number of times I refer to it . . .

Quite a lot of light flak along the route, but very heavy stuff flung up over Gelsenkirchen: but having said that, it didn't appear to me to be nearly as heavy as it was when we visited there on 13 June (God! that was all of five weeks ago; our eighth one and now we're on to our twentieth). It could be that I only *thought* it wasn't as heavy, that earlier effort over the place being our first German raid and in any case now being more used to having flak bursting all around us. Anyway, it was heavy enough to tear a large number of holes out of the Lanc. (Was illogical enough to feel anger when I examined them. Imagine, actually trying to wreck beautiful 'B' for Baker!)

That target got well and truly plastered. Those fires! Like some Dante-visioned Hades. As we approached Gelsenkirchen we saw perhaps half a dozen heavy fires raging in different parts of the city (maybe where the oil refinery is, maybe not) which had been started by the first wave. Fires which were all converging on each other to such an extent that, by the time *we* were over the target, it was simply a sea of leaping flames. I dropped the load right in the middle of it.

Can understand now these stories we hear from time to time about aircrew baling out over a city which they have destroyed like this and being strung up by civilians from the nearest lamp post. Could be true enough.

On looking back at my record of our earlier attack of Gelsenkirchen, I see I expressed the faint niggling at the back of my mind re women and children. No faint niggling this time; didn't even give it a thought. Wonder, as I write this, if I'm becoming hardened or am just not allowing myself even to contemplate the number of civilians these bombs of mine must have killed. And it is: 'must have' – you can't drop a 4,000 pounder and eighteen 500s and fool yourself that the only harm you did was to destroy either part of an oil refinery or some uninhabited buildings. Anyway, the Germans are doing the same thing to us.

The main briefing, I must record, was just as intense and detailed as the earlier one for the same target. Routes were slightly different, but not much more.

And about the only humour around was when one pilot observed plaintively that he had bombed that bloody oil refinery only about five weeks ago and was told that if he and his oppos had bombed the bloody place *properly* that time we wouldn't all be having to go back there tonight. He accompanied his nodded acceptance of this with a request for a promise that if we knocked out the oil refinery completely tonight we wouldn't have to go back a *third* time. His request was ignored.

I had thought that the German night fighter controller's job was only to guide his flock on to us. but this character over the Gelsenkirchen area extended his remit to include quite a harangue (in a most beautifully modulated English accent; probably acquired at Cambridge or Oxford). He told us that there were no military installations in Gelsenkirchen and that we were killing innocent women and children, that when we were shot down by the valiant Luftwaffe they (the Luftwaffe presumably) couldn't be responsible for our safety at the hands of those we were bombing so indiscriminately. He then went on to call us, among other things: 'English Terror Flyers'. I asked WOP to put me on the air for a quick second. Vernon said no, to cut it out, but I persisted. When Dunn said OK, I was on, I pointed out to the controller that there were Scots as well as English attending the proceedings. A pause: then a somewhat petulant: 'Oh, very well: Scots Terror Flyers also.' I felt much happier at this inclusion: one doesn't like all the credit to go to the Sassenach . . .

But am hellishly tired: which is why I haven't recorded any losses we might have had – can't be bothered going down to the interrogation room to find out.

Went to bed but couldn't sleep because of my mind dwelling on

F/Lt Muirhead

Lancaster in flight

*Imperial War Museum*

Lancasters at dawn

*Imperial War Museum*

An RAF bomber crew being interrogated by a WAAF officer after a raid on Boulogne. Great damage was done to E-boats, R-boats and minesweepers in the harbour.

*Flight magazine, 29 June 1944*

Crew, reading from left to right:
Sgt. Griggs, Engineer; F/O Muirhead, Bomb aimer; Sgt. Dunn, Wireless operator; Sgt. Norman, Navigator; Sgt. Cartwright, Rear gunner; P/O Horsefall, Mid-upper gunner; F/O Vernon, Pilot.

L.7540 44 SQDN. JAN 42, 83. 207 CON. FLTS - 1654 CU., 5 L.F.S S.O.C APL. 44.
14TH A/C IN 83 SQDN CODE:- OL - U - UNCLE - EX KM. ? 44 SQDN.
BATCH L.7527 to L.7549

Bomb sections being loaded into a Lancaster bomber prior to a bombing operation

*Imperial War Museum*

12 Squadron Badge

626 Squadron Badge

Not the recommended way to land a PT17A trainer! (The author failed pilot training in Arizona in 1942)

A recent picture of Campbell Muirhead

that horrific 4,000 pounder I'd dropped on Gelsenkirchen. So got up again to enter something about it in this diary. The bomb had a delayed action device on it: when I fused it in the Lanc I really primed it so that it didn't go off when it hit the deck: neither when moved would it detonate: but the moving of it, however slight, activated the delayed action mechanism so that about 20 minutes later it exploded. Nice, pleasant, friendly world we live in, eh? (One of the Intelligence types told us that the Germans get concentration camp prisoners to move those monstrous things: promise them food for doing so. Yes, a nice, pleasant, friendly world all right). Back to bed again now. Still got ten to do. Hope no more like this.

No, still can't sleep. So might as well keep on writing until the Mess starts serving breakfast. Well, that's two-thirds of the tour over (always was quite good at arithmetic!) and we've been very lucky having had only two of that lot over Germany. Looks, however, as if all the rest might be over the Reich; a reflection which keeps one rather subdued.

But the war's getting on. The Allied Armies seem to be doing OK in France, now pressing on beyond Caen and inflicting heavy casualities on the Wehrmacht; and in the East the Russians evidently have the upper hand and are inflicting even heavier losses. Maybe Hitler's biggest mistake – apart from fighting a war on two fronts – was to build the Luftwaffe almost entirely as a tactical force (to support his armies) instead of a strategic one with heavy bombers which could get at Russia's war factories, etc. behind the Urals. In Italy too the Germans are hard pressed: and we have the 'U' boat menace under control. Wonder when the end of the European War will come. Forecasts that it could be over by Christmas (but I seem to remember such forecasts back in 1939!) And after it, what then? Off to the Far East maybe. Quite likely, because the Japs are proving a hard nut to crack and, even when the full weight of the Americans and ourselves is directed towards them, will fight to the last man. Imagine the Lancs and the Fortresses over Japan and the damage they will do to the flimsy Jap houses. Trouble will be, I suppose, finding bases from which they can operate. Then after Japan gets the chop – which it most assuredly will – what then? Will it be peace, perfect peace? Said that after WW I, that it was the war to end all wars, and it wasn't. Neither will this one be; already here and there you find people nodding darkly that it will end with Russia being so powerful in Europe that we'll have to be on our guard against domination by Stalin.

God, what a chronicle of despair! Better leave off before it gets worse. In any case, breakfast time coming up. Maybe after it, if my services are not in demand, I'll return here and try to get some sleep. Trouble is, right now, I'm no longer tired: could be that all my gloomy foreboding has wakened me up!

**Later**

The breakfast was excellent – baked beans on toast. Very fond of baked beans so had a second helping. Three cups of coffee too. Coffee usually keeps me awake at nights, but I sat down in an easy chair in the ante-room to read a paper and almost before I knew it I'd dozed off. Was awakened rudely by Horsfall who, after referring to me as a lazy sod, suggested a nice little run round the airfield would be just the thing to waken me up. Besides, he felt I wasn't taking enough exercise these days and such a run, in addition to waking me up, would be extremely beneficial to me. Horsfall is much more athletic than I am, and much stronger and fitter, so I could not offer him the violence I would have wished to. I therefore had to resort to telling him precisely what he could do with his 'nice little run round the airfield'. He took no offence at this invitation and walked away slowly shaking his head from side to side.

**20 July 1944**

Feel like writing something about this room I have here at Wickenby. In a hut, of course: and just a few yards from the Mess. I'm lucky in that it's rather a large room and I have it all to myself. Contains a hospital-type issue RAF bed, a small chest of drawers, and a bedside table; also a miniscule carpet. Managed to acquire a small table and chair from the NAAFI (No Ambition And Fuckall Interest) which I think the manager has now given up looking for; this I refer to as my 'writing desk'. It's nice being on your toddy, not having to talk when you don't feel like it, staying up writing if you *do* feel like it, getting into the pit whenever you feel like it, and so on.

But returned from an op to find that they had shoved another two beds, two side-tables and two chests of drawers into it. I had company. Two P/Os. One from the Irish Free State, not unsurprisingly called Paddy; the other from Cardiff and, surprise, surprise, answers to the name of Taffy. And to them, of course, I'm Jock. (Given up trying to tell the English that I have a name other than Jock: only way to get them out of calling me Jock would be to refer to all of them as 'Limey', which would be impracticable.)

They're crewed up together, Paddy being pilot and Taffy navigator: rest of crew are sergeants. A bit nervous; understandably so, because they haven't done their first yet. How many had I done? I tell them. To their next question I say yes – *shit* scared: until airborne, then it's not so bad. (But when I say this the looks on their faces reflect that they think I'm taking the mick.) I invite them up to the ante-room where I confuse their confirmed impression of the Scots by buying them a pint. Vernon and Horsfall are there. I introduce them as the worst bloody pilot in the whole of 12 Squadron and a mid-upper gunner who couldn't hit a FW190 if it impaled itself on his guns. They see those footprints up one wall, along the ceiling and down the other (some other crew's been at the game again) and say are we all round the bend? We reply that indeed we are and that it's high time they bought another round. Which they do.

On the way back to our room Paddy asked if I had any real tips to offer. I said none, really, except that if you even *thought* you were being tailed to corkscrew like hell, but to get back into the middle of the stream once you'd shaken him off. So important to keep right in the middle of the stream.

**Added later**

Paddy and Taffy came with us to Stuttgart on 24 July. They didn't come back with us. Grim that: for your first op you get a bastard like Stuttgart where you maybe have a slight chance if you're experienced, but where you have virtually no chance if you're a sprog crew. (Yet, having said that, many an experienced crew has bought it on what looked like a simple daylight over France.)

They've now removed the two beds etc. from my room and I'm on my own once more. Paddy and Taffy – I never knew their names. With a bit of luck they're maybe now in the bag. But to get it on your very first – oh, Christ!

| | |
|---|---|
| *Op. No. 21* | *20-21 July 1944* |
| *Target* | Marshalling yards at COURTERAI (BELGIUM) |
| *A/C 'B'* | *Load* 11 x 1,000lbs.<br>4 x 500lbs. |
| *Take off* | 23:35 hrs. *Duration* 3:35 hrs. |
| *Height* | 11,000ft. |
| *Flak* | Nil |
| *S/Ls* | Nil |
| *E/A* | None sighted but evidently around |

Target area appeared very quiet when first wave was over it. But the second wave, of which we were part, encountered quite a bit of fighter opposition. Many fighter flares dropped. We did some corkscrewing and were not attacked.

But we don't get off scotfree from those comparatively quiet efforts on marshalling yards. Nine missing from this raid including three from Wickenby. The entire night's ops, which included raids on the Ruhr, buzz-bombs sites, etc. cost the RAF 31 a/c missing. That's over 200 blokes. Not all killed, of course, but for the majority it's the chop.

A sad, sad, note: our old friend 'H' for Harry bought it on this one. Old 'H' for Harry who saw us through four of our earlier ops. Truly, feel like weeping. Also for the crew – their very first operational flight. This old game, I suppose: the older, almost clapped-out, kites go to the sprog crews, the powers-that-be reckoning that green, inexperienced aircrew are more likely than anybody else to get themselves shot down and that, this being the case, it's going to be an old Lanc that buys it, not a brand-new effort equipped with $H_2S$ and such-like. Brutal, but I suppose it has to be. After all, that applied to us also at the end of May/early June.

A different atmosphere on this one. There we were, after Gelsenkirchen, absolutely convinced that from now on it was the Reich for us and that we had kissed goodbye to those easier French jobs. And all becoming unwound on discovering that we were back on the marshalling yards efforts (in this case a Belgian rather than a French target, but there is no difference, really).

Too much chat when heading for the enemy coast all because of this unwinding. I contributed to it by adding my piece that chat on the intercom meant less vigilance and that it was high time everybody dried up. Vernon took the hint and ordered no talking unless necessary. It was about thirty seconds later that Horsfall, obviously having spotted what he thought was an enemy fighter, bawled out:

'Corkscrew, corkscrew,' and added: 'For f . . . s sake!' His extra three-word exhortation was quite unnecessary because even before it Vernon had put her into a headlong dive to starboard. But, although it maybe sounds self-satisfied to be writing so, it was complete justification of my earlier bit about less vigilance if chatting. Better to be self-satisfied than dead . . .

**Later**

Forgot to moan that we nearly got bombed by a 'friendly' aircraft on that one. Not quite on the run-up when Horsfall yells out that there's a Lanc right above us with its bomb doors open. (It must have been almost on top of us if he could see that.) We alter course slightly to take us out from beneath it so that when he drops his load none of it will hit us on its way down. In fact, quite a few of our aircraft have been struck by bombs from above. Not surprising considering the numbers which are usually milling around over the target. Don't think the bombs actually explode, but can cause problems . . .

**22 July 1944**

A Mustang landed at Wickenby today so we went out to where the fighter was parked to have a look at it. Certainly beautiful lines. The fitter who was working on the kite told us it belonged to some visiting Group Captain who used it as his personal chariot. When I mentioned to him that this was a waste of an immaculate fighter he said not this one – it was powered by a Yank (Allison, I think he said) engine, not the British Rolls-Royce Merlin. Evidently the RAF had ordered some of these fighters a year or so back but, after testing in dog-fights against Spits, had decided they definitely would not match up to the MEs or the FWs. So they'd farmed them out to some Station Commanders for personal use. The Engineering Officer on one of these stations was so impressed by the aerodynamical qualities of the Mustang that, with permission, he took out its American engine, replaced it with a RR Merlin, and arranged for it and a Spitfire to 'have a go at each other'. The Mustang proved itself the superior. The Americans were quick on the ball: in no time they had a licence to build Merlins in the USA: and in next to no time did they fit them to their Mustangs. The salvation of the Fortresses over Germany; these Mustangs, with their drop tanks, can escort the bombers all over Europe. Yes, the salvation of the USAAF daylight bombers and the virtual destruction of what is left of the Luftwaffe daylight fighter force.

On the subject of Fortresses over Germany, we hear they are encountering jet-fighters now. Hard to believe that an aircraft can stooge around the sky without a propellor: and fuelled not by petrol but by something akin to kerosene. But it could be quite true: there's an entire page in the current issue of *Flight* magazine by Gloster intimating that they are the designers and builders of the first jet-propelled aircraft in Great Britain. So if we have them, the Germans probably likewise. Heavens, we'll have jet *bombers* next!

**22 July 1944**

Was told of a very sad happening. It concerned the raid on the marshalling yards at Courterai. At the briefing, a pilot had reported one crew member absent – his rear-gunner, who had gone sick. That crew was consequently about to be scrubbed when a French-Canadian F/S air-gunner volunteered to go in the sick gunner's place. This French-Canadian had done two full operational tours, his second one being from Wickenby, and was all ready for his posting back to Canada. However, he could not stay away from this briefing, although he was no longer operational, and had talked his way into the Briefing Room. The Gunnery Leader wasn't too keen to let him go. I'm not so sure of his reasons: one could have been that the crew the French-Canadian would be flying with was a truly sprog one, having but recently arrived at Wickenby: the other might have been that he (the Gunnery Leader) was half-way through his own second tour and was only too happy to jump in when an air-gunner called off sick. But the French-Canadian F/S persisted, adding that it was only a French trip lasting 3½ hours and, after what he had been through, would be a piece of cake.

At this stage, I must admit I nearly stood up to shout: 'Don't go, you silly bastard – you're asking for it.' I *nearly* did: but, of course, I didn't.

Also, of course, that Lanc didn't return. As I've noted about Op. No. 21, there was quite a bit of fighter opposition and this relatively unskilled crew must have bought it then, being one of the three missing from Wickenby.

But to do 60 and then volunteer for one more! I hope his folks never find out. Which is the reason I've not recorded his name. I am quite certain this record of mine will never see the light of day – and as I write it this is certainly not my intention – but one never knows: after all, if I get the chop, I'll have no control over what happens to it, will I?

Wouldn't get *me* volunteering for an extra one when, and if, I make the 30. And I could swear the same goes for the rest of our crew. God, you're *begging* for the chop if you do even that one over your tour.

Have been in Cartwright's turrent. That rear turret is the least enviable position in the Lanc. An attack almost inevitably comes from behind and the rear gunner receives the full cannon blast. Sometimes he's the only one who gets it, the Lanc having started corkscrewing immediately on the attack and thereby escaping but, in so many cases, too late to save the gunner. Cartwright makes light of it saying that if he has to be hosed out of the turret on return to base – as has happened on some occasions – at least he'll know nothing about it. Some rear gunners receive dreadful injuries in the attacks and, even if the aircraft manages to make it back to base, are often almost impossible to extricate from the turret. It is difficult enough to get out of in any event, the exit being so small. Certainly the most dangerous position in the aircraft. And to reflect that, back in Canada, when the bomb aimer's course looked like being a long time in coming up, I thought of changing to the Air Gunner's course, which was more immediate, in case the war was over before I got back to UK!

The mid-upper turret isn't all that easy to get out of either, particularly with Horsfall being so big, but is a piece of cake compared to that rear effort.

My front turret I can get out of easily – no difficulty at all there. And if I'm in my bomb aimer's compartment I can get out of that Lanc quicker than anybody. Because I lie on top of the escape hatch: one pull and it's up and all I have to do is to fall out. Out and down. Have one great fear. Which is that, in the panic which will be enveloping me if we have to bale out, I'll forget to clip on my parachute pack first. Told it has happened.

**23 July 1944**

Informed by Norman that a spirited rendering of 'The Airmen's Lament' got under way in the Sergeants' Mess last night after the consumption of more than the odd pint.

Occasionally, in our own Mess, there have been attempts to launch this subtle piece of Air Force folklore (folklore only on the grounds that it is said to have originated in the Royal Flying Corps: which is rather a nasty allegation to make against what I am sure was otherwise a very fine body of men: am equally sure that some research could trace its origin to the brown jobs). Any such attempts have always been throttled at birth as against the possibility that some WAAF officer might come in to the ante-room during the progress of 'The Lament' causing acute embarrassment all round.

For it is crudeness itself. Starts off innocuously enough:

'An airman told me before he died
And I've no reason to believe he lied'

The WAAF officer could have walked in at that stage and, especially if newly joined, could well have equated it to something akin to a Sunday school choir getting under way. But disillusionment would have come immediately after: because the song goes on to explain, in clinical detail, that a certain section of the wife's anatomy was so generous that satisfaction was not to be her lot in life leading the airman to construct a contraption which, he was sure, would rectify this sad state of marital affairs. Once completed, the device was activated by steam. The action of the mechanism, as the song progresses, is illustrated by the singers with a vigorous movement of arms: and usually, when the machine has completed the purpose for which it was constructed, someone manages to effect a high falsetto voice indicating, on the part of the wife, that she is now more than prepared to rest content. The tempo then slows as tragedy strikes: for, alas, the airman's lack of mechanical skills is revealed in that he has omitted to include in his specification a means of actually stopping his otherwise brilliant effort. With truly horrendous results. Which concludes 'The Airman's Lament'. Except for a most blasphemous exhortation which I hope none of our devil-dodgers has ever heard.

This was the work of art which Norman told me got under way in the Sergeants' Mess last night. Sung, with visual accompaniment, by a large mob of aircrew, who, to give them their due, had first chased out the WAAF sergeants some of whom, according to Norman, were most reluctant to depart and had to be threatened with knicker removing. ('The daftest, possible threat you could have made to *one* of them,' he amplified. 'It encouraged her to stay.')

The choir was just recounting the disaster scene and its dreadful results when in walked the Station Warrant Officer. He was accompanied by three WAAF sergeants who had just arrived at Wickenby. They got the full blast. I asked Norman why the SWO, who must have heard the singing from outside, didn't delay his entry, but he said the fellow was slightly deaf. He must have been: and more than slightly.

Norman concluded that the unexpected and sudden entry of the SWO and the two WAAF sergeants meant that they hadn't been able to finish 'The Lament' with the obligatory blasphemous exhortation. I gather it rather spoiled the evening for him.

**24 July 1944**

Could kick myself! I 'phoned Ann quite regularly from here – mainly to let her know I'm OK. Hadn't 'phoned for the last few days and had determined to do so this evening (the sky being rather overcast and, in my opinion, the likelihood of an op being laid on therefore quite faint). Thought I'd have a cup of coffee before I did so. And wish I hadn't, because half-way through my cup the Tannoy blared forth ordering all Operation Crews to the Briefing Room at 17:00 hrs.

The second that announcement is made, all non-military outside lines are cut: there is no way anybody at Wickenby can get on to the Post Office network. The unit itself is sealed off: you can be stood-down, sick, about to go on leave – anything you like – but you cannot get out of Wickenby. (In this respect, I note that even official RAF traffic does not seem to leave the unit: although I suppose there will be exceptions to this.)

Ann will probably be concerned: yes, I do wish I hand't had that cup of coffee. Especially as it wasn't very clever . . .

| | |
|---|---|
| *Op. No. 22* | *24-25 July 1944* |
| *Target* | STUTTGART |
| *A/C 'B'* | *Load* 1x2,000lbs.<br>12xJ-type cluster incendiaries |
| *Take off* | 21:30 hrs. *Duration* 8:25 hrs. |
| *Height* | 19,000ft. |
| *Flak* | Light (owing to heavy cloud) |
| *S/Ls* | Do. |
| *E/A* | All over the place. Saw interceptions take place even before we'd hit the enemy coast – they seemed to be coming out to sea to meet us: indeed, we were stalked while still over the water but by violent corkscrewing were able to ditch him. Another interception when only a few miles inland: saw a flurry of tracer just slightly to starboard, but it looked like two-way stuff (that Lanc would have been much better corkscrewing rather than trying to fight it out). Someone else coming up behind us shortly after that – could have been the same fighter, of course – so off corkscrewing again. Didn't see anybody buying it, though, but that could have been because of the heavy cloud all around us<br>Bombing of Stuttgart not as concentrated as it might have been – again owing to the heavy cloud. Purely an area bash this: nothing military about it. Saw what looked like a ME110 when leaving the target. Was flying on the same course as ourselves and at about the same height. Some heavy cloud nearby so we slid into it |

Odd how, despite the heavy cloud over Stuttgart, the Target Indicators seemed to be brighter than ever before. These are usually dropped by the Pathfinders and are, in effect, bombs which explode at a set height above the target releasing ignited pyrotechnic candles which, in turn, slowly cascade earthwards spreading as they do so. When they land they form wide circles of bright fire of varying colours, easily seen from the air. If there's a Master of Ceremonies present he will instruct by wireless which colours to bomb. There may be circles of reds and you're told to drop your loads on that colour. Then this almost inevitable 'creep-back' could occur as a result of bomb aimers releasing their bombs prematurely and causing the approach to the target to bear the brunt of the attack rather than the target proper. In such cases the MC might drop a fresh set of TIs – say coloured green – and intimate that the reds were now to be ignored and that the greens only were to be used as aiming points.

But they were certainly brighter than I've ever seen them before. Probably new models with more powerful candles: they're always 'improving' on any items which will hasten the destruction of the Reich that was, according to Adolf, going to last for a thousand years . . .

Forgot to record above that I got a fleeting glimpse of what looked like a Heinkel 111 flying through the beam of a searchlight. Could have been mistaken though as these bombers are now obsolete and have been withdrawn from active daylight service against the RAF. Possibly they use the odd one at nights packed with jamming gear: or maybe to drop flares to guide the night fighters to the bomber stream. Anyway, it brought back to me a brief memory of the beginning of the War when the Luftwaffe made an abortive daylight raid on the Forth Bridge using this type of aircraft and one was shot down near Humbie, just outside Edinburgh. Cycled to Humbie to see the Heinkel. Never for a moment thought, as I surveyed the wrecked bomber, that the next time I saw a Heinkel it would be over the Reich itself . . .

| | |
|---|---|
| *Op. No. 23* | *25-26 July 1944* |
| *Target* | STUTTGART |
| *A/C 'B'* | *Load* 1x2,000lbs.<br>12xJ-type cluster incendiaries |
| *Take off* | 21:00 hrs. *Duration* 9:00 hrs. |
| *Height* | 14,000ft. |
| *Flak* | Moderate, considering it was a German city |
| *S/Ls* | Not many – too cloudy |
| *E/A* | As opposed to last night, very few. No doubt German Control didn't reckon on us bombing Stuttgart two nights running and vectored their N/Fs elsewhere. There were quite a few fighter flares along the route and all sorts of coloured things dropped on us, but that, I think, is about all – the Luftwaffe was certainly not out in force |

Massive fires this time (evidently we didn't do a good enough job last night, which is why we had to return). The fires multiplied as we approached the target and each wave of Lancs deposited its 2,000 pounder and its clusters of incendiaries. An out and out area bash, of course. We could see the fires, despite the amount of cloud, for well over 100 miles after leaving the target.

Another long, tiring effort alleviated only by the R/G dropping a bottle of urine over the target. While awaiting take-off we had been approached by an airman carrying a lemonade bottle full of a yellow-coloured liquid. He said he'd taken a bet with his pals that he'd piss on the Third Reich. As he wasn't aircrew they'd reckoned it was like taking candy from a kid. Would we do him a favour and drop it? When Cartwright told us he was dropping the bottle, it was Vernon who was first with the inevitable remark: 'Hope that fucking bottle doesn't hurt some poor bastard down there.'

Quite a muttering when, at Briefing, the cover over the Order of Battle was whipped off to reveal the name of the target. 'But we were there only *last* bloody night,' complained a pilot in the front row. He was congratulated on such a feat of memory and informed that if Stuttgart wasn't flattened on this effort he might find himself over the place for even a third night.

But Germany two nights running. I think all of us in the crew are now almost reconciled to Germany for our remaining seven. Lucky seven? Could be.

Sometimes on a long flight, when you've done all you have to do for the meantime, you find yourself falling into a somewhat reflective mood. Fell into such a mood on that second Stuttgart effort. Don't know what causes it – maybe the dull droning of the engines, maybe the fact that you've got that oxygen mask clamped over your face, maybe even because, despite the fact that there are seven of you in the kite, you are alone in your bombing compartment or front turret and feel isolated. Could be all these put together: could be that you're simply plain tired.

But the further we flew away from England out across the North Sea the deeper these reflections became. Soon we'd be over Germany. Age 23 and your sole purpose in life, apart from trying to keep it, is to convey that bastard 2,000 pounder of High Explosive plus the J-type cannisters crammed with their dreadful incendiaries to Stuttgart. The HE strikes first, tearing buildings apart; the incendiaries come next setting aflame the resulting masses of rubble. That's what's awaiting them at Stuttgart: brought there by me and hundreds of others like me. Also wonder whether the sirens have already sounded there – once you're well into Germany their Controllers are able to calculate what your likely target is: and whether people are already cowering in air raid shelters waiting for the fearful onslaught. People, that's who you're after as well as industry, houses, schools, anything that will burn: men, probably mostly elderly the fit being in the Forces, women maybe some of them factory workers but probably most of them older. And children. Children of all ages. I know the Germans brought it upon themselves. I know nobody can stop it until they surrender. But, God, it's a terrible killing time.

Almost glad when some event around us jerks you away from such a gloomy reflecting. You really can't afford such brooding.

**Later**

Just remembered to add that this is the first time I've seen one of these decoy targets the Intelligence types keep on nattering about. Came up on it about five or six miles north of Stuttgart, practically on our track. From the air it really does look like a burning city – you can see outlines of streets, squares, what could be buildings, all coming up in bright flame. And up from around this also came some flak. As we approached, the Germans fired some spoof markers in the centre of the conflagration (by means of rockets, probably). They were exactly the same as the Target Indicators being dropped by the first wave on Stuttgart itself; greens surrounded by reds. But they seemed to burn rather brighter than ours. Had I been on my first German op and never seen from the air a city burning I might have been tempted to drop my load on the decoy target. But I know by now exactly what a German city looks like when it is being laid waste and so the 2,000 pounder and the incendiaries remained reserved for Stuttgart instead of being dropped in the middle of fields some miles away from it.

**27 July 1944**

A few days' stand-down so decided to go to London. On my own, Vernon having elected to look up a girl-friend in Ipswich, Horsfall away to visit some rugby club in the wilds of Yorkshire, and the sergeants asserting that they were simply going to have three days in their Mess spending their time eating, sleeping and drinking. (In that order, too – they're not a boozy crowd.)

So cycled to Lincoln and put the Raleigh into the left luggage: after a struggle, the porter doubting whether it could really be termed a 'parcel'. But I think he was simply trying to assert whatever authority he had because often I've booked that bike into the left luggage.

Then a dreadful crawl from Lincoln to London. Seems to me the LNER is becoming somewhat clapped out. No wonder – I don't think any repairs of track or rolling stock have been done since 1939.

London heaving with uniforms. Every uniform under the sun. Well, every uniform except that of the enemy. (Yet, I'll wager that you could put on Wehrmacht uniform and stroll around Trafalgar Square unmolested: unless you were unfortunate enough to be accosted by some Poles!)

Found it all a bit boring. Was going to go to the Windmill, but there was a long queue and I couldn't be bothered standing in it.

And didn't fancy the cinema: seemed to be so many war films around and these, at that moment, were not exactly my cup of tea.

Knew a girl who worked in the War Office so called in there: but she was off sick.

Yes, on the boring side: and found myself really just wanting to get back to Wickenby, to get on with the tour and, with lots of luck, to finish it.

But decided to visit a pub first. Bumped into an Australian bomb aimer there; literally, because I spilled his pint for him. Told him to stop calling me a pommie bastard – that I was a Scots one – and thereafter got on famously with him. Maybe a bit too famously because when we left the pub he expressed his sincere intention of returning to Wickenby and completing my tour of ops on my behalf.

After ditching the Aussie I started walking rather aimlessly. By chance I came across the South African Legation. I had run out of fags and there didn't seem to be any shops around for miles: so, on the spur of the moment, I decided to go in to see if there were any SA fags going. The chap I met was very pleasant. I explained that I was born in South Africa, indeed that my birth certificate was in Afrikaans, that I had run out of fags and could he help? He replied that in the event they had no South African fags at present, that he smoked Gold Flake anyway and would I like one? Over the fag, and a cup of coffee, we chatted away about the war.

As I left, he handed me a form. 'Consider it,' he said. 'All expenses paid – first class – for you and your wife – to South Africa. Retain your present rank, of course. Would be glad to have you.'

It was an application form to join the South African Air Force . . .

Sgt. Wells, a bomb aimer in 626 Squadron, who evidently accompanied us on quite a few of the same targets, is still chuckling over an incident involving some of the Aussie sergeants who had indulged in some crafty sheep stealing. On a foggy night, when there had not been any flying, he and the other NCOs in his crew had been lying around in their hut (which was on the outskirts of the airfield) feeling bored when suddenly the door was banged open and an Aussie sergeant charged in to invite them to come for a good nosh up. They followed him through the fog to the Aussie's hut from which, as they approached, they could detect a delightful aroma of roasting meat. On entering, Sgt. Wells found himself wondering why the hut hadn't gone up in flames: both the heavy cast iron stoves were red hot to halfway up the chimney pipe and joints of meat where hanging all around them being grilled, the fat dropping all over the hearths and the floor boards. About 50 airmen were jammed into the hut, all eating away with expressions of delight. He was told that some of the Aussies had been over the fence at the adjoining field, caught a couple of sheep then slaughtered and butchered them being careful to bury all the non-edible parts so that no evidence remained. Sgt. Wells joined in, eating with bare hands: said it was one of the best meals he'd ever had.

But it's not only Aussie aircrew who get up to tricks. There's an Airborne unit based outside Horncastle and very proud of their Regimental signboard beautifully painted in maroon and blue and complete with Pegasus and Para badge. Until one evening it disappeared: an evening during which several RAF NCOs from 626 Squadron had been their guests. Some time later the paras were invited to a guest night in the 626 Sergeants' Mess at Wickenby. On entering, the first item their eyes fell upon was their own Regimental signboard displayed in a prominent position. Understand that only a liberal handing out of booze on the part of the RAF prevented an outbreak of hostilities there and then. In the event, they didn't take their board back with them. Either because they were so tight they'd forgotten all about it or because they'd already had a new one painted.

Always find plenty of things to keep me occupied here at Wickenby; apart from all this writing.

Today, was down at the Rifle range: have always fancied myself with a Lee-Enfield and knocked up quite a good score. They also had some of those old .300 Ross rifles which, I think, came from

Canada. Made for the 1914-1918 War, but the main rifle issued here in 1939/40 to defend ourselves in the event of invasion. Some state of affairs. Anyway, knocked up quite a good score with the Ross, despite that circle it has for a rear sight. On to a revolver next, but dreadful with it: don't think I could hit a door from ten yards with a revolver. As an officer I'm entitled to draw a revolver for my 'own personal use'. Nobody has defined exactly: 'own personal use', but some aircrew carry a revolver on ops. Don't think that's very wise: to produce a revolver on being shot down (and why produce it if no intention of using?) is simply asking for trouble. Me, if shot down, up go my hands to the first soldier who even *looks* like pointing his rifle in my direction! No, a revolver is just not on as far as I am concerned.

Before I left the range, the NCO in charge of it asked me if I wanted to throw a Mills bomb or two. Maybe he was joking, but from the look on his face when I declined the offer I received the impression that he wasn't.

On way back to my billet and passing Intelligence Officer's hide-out remembered he had invited me to look in to see some additions to what he is always describing as his 'toys'. The 'toys' are various gadgets to help you escape shortly after being shot down. They would be of no use once you were in the hands of the Luftwaffe or the Wehrmacht whose Intelligence types would know all about these items and who, on their first professional search, would most probably unearth them. These are designed to help you get away if your first arrest is at the hands of a German or French policeman who could not be expected to know of their existence and who would not search you for them before locking you up in his police station cell. Already, I had a comb which, when broken, revealed a file with which I could saw away at a bar of a prison cell. Similarly, I had a pencil which also broke to reveal a file (presumably to saw away at two bars simultaneously). His new 'toys' were (a) a RAF uniform button, the top of which unscrewed to reveal a compass and (b) a pen which could be pulled open to reveal the same. So now I have two files and two compasses to assist me in any possible future breakout from a German or French local civilian jail.

Then just nearing the billets when a Flying Fortress swept low across the runway. Horsfall and Vernon came out to see it land. It taxied to one of the nearer bays so the three of us walked out to have a look at it. When the crew had climbed out, Vernon spoke to the captain who seemed quite surprised to find an American flying with the RAF (despite the fact that there are quite a few doing this). Was Vernon's turn to be surprised when on asking why the Fortress had landed at Wickenby, he was informed that it was getting on towards dusk and that they 'couldn't fly in the dark'. Which seems to be perfectly true: the Americans are day flyers and are not trained for night flying; to be caught by the darkness when airborne could be disastrous. The American pilot showed us around his 'ship'. Think what impressed some of us most was the fact that the B17 had fitted ashtrays. The gunners envied the .5 machine guns and wished the Lanc had them instead of our .303s. They scoffed at my observation that *our* chief means of evading fighters was by corkscrewing, not slugging it out with weapons, and that therefore whether our guns were .5s or .303s was not really all that important. I could well be wrong, though.

The Yank pilot and his navigator, both of whom were First Lieutenants, came back with us to the Mess where we bought them a drink, the rest of their crew being conducted to the Sergeants' Mess. A room with two beds was soon found for them. After dinner the American pilot gave Vernon a carton of Lucky Strikes (not that we're the least bit short of fags, but all Yanks seem to have thousands of them). Vernon shared them around, but these toasted efforts are not everybody's taste.

Yes, as I said when I started this entry, you can always find plenty of things to keep you occupied at Wickenby . . .

**Later**

Checked up on the Lancaster's performance compared to that of the Fortress. The Lanc can carry 10,000lbs of bombs for 2,250 miles (or 14,000lbs for 1,660 miles) while the Fortress can carry only 4,000lbs for slightly over 2,000 miles. So, as regards bomb-load and distance that it can be carried, the Lanc is by far the superior. But there it ends. The Lanc carries but eight .303 machines guns while the Fortress carries twelve .5 machine guns (which give it all-round fire). And it's these heavier guns fired from the Fortresses in formation which afford them *some* protection from the Luftwaffe day fighters which manage to get through the escorting Allied fighters. In a similar position the more lightly armed Lancs would be dead ducks.

Got to hand it to the Yanks. Their first daylight attacks, unescorted by fighters, brought with them dreadful losses, but they persisted. And now, with fighter cover all the way to their targets in Germany it is they who are clawing the Luftwaffe day fighter force out of the sky. For that they have the immaculate Mustang to thank. In the past if an attacking bomber force was lucky enough to have fighter cover with it, these fighters, by virtue of having to engage so far from base, were so often inferior in performance to the defending fighters. But not so with the Mustang. From material available in the Intelligence Section it seems pretty certain that this fighter with its Merlin engine is superior in most (but not all) fields to its two main opponents over Germany – the latest models of the ME109 and the FW190.

Don't have to be all that bright to conclude that if the Americans were not engaging, and destroying, so much of the Luftwaffe day fighter forces, there would be a hell of a lot more available to defend against *us* on our night efforts. So we're all for the Yanks . . .

**30 July 1944**

De Havilland Mosquito also landed here today so nipped out on my bike to have a look at it. Wouldn't think an aircraft made of balsa wood could be as perfect as the Mossie. It's a bomber that can drop a 'blockbuster' on Berlin; a fighter which can hold its own with most Luftwaffe stuff (especially at night when Mossies come along in the bomber stream and stalk the ME110s which are stalking us); a reconnaissance plane which, unarmed, can outstrip any pursuer with ease. It's a perfect all-rounder, the Mossie.

Thinking of the obsolete aircraft we possessed when the war started – dreadful efforts like the Fairey Battle with which 12 Squadron was equipped – and comtemplating beauties like the Mosquito (and, of course, the Lanc) makes you agree with the accuracy of the statement that the air force built up by a nation with which to launch a war becomes obsolete in a very short space of time and is superseded by that of the nation which has to start practically from scratch. It's certainly true. If the aggressor doesn't knock the other out first. Which didn't happen with us, hence magnificent aircraft like this Mossie.

**30 July 1944**

Detailed for a daylight bombing exercise: also to practice $H_2S$. Heavens, you'd think we were getting enough of that over France, without having to go and dump stuff on some inoffensive Bombing Range which never did anybody any harm. (Don't envy the airmen who have to man these ranges – admittedly from some distance away – in order to plot the hits: or, as in the case of some of the bomb aimers I know around here, the misses.)

But it's to be for only a couple of hours or so and everybody's in quite good fettle as we climb aboard the dispersal truck. It's also a nice, sunny day and nobody's going to be throwing anything up at us, so once we are dropped at the Lanc a certain amount of fooling around is on the programme, if Horsfall, never able to forget he's an RAF rugby cap, gets his way: he suggests a quick game of rugger and to this end drops his parachute pack in one place, his flying helmet a few feet along from it, and indicates these are the posts.

This proposal meets with no enthusiasm from anybody and I return him a two-finger salute which I feel I'm still owing him for something or another. Such uncooperation means absolutely nothing to Horsfall who, no doubt, had encountered much more passive resistance during his pre-war regular days as a Physical

Training Instructor. He runs through the bunch of us grabbing Dunn's forage cap in passing. He brakes about 10 yards away, turns, informs us that Dunn's forage cap is the ball and that he is going to score a try between the two 'posts' he's just set up, adding that a shower like us certainly couldn't stop him. At which he charges right into the centre of us. Whose leg trips him up I do not know, but I think its Cartwright's. He falls flat on his face. We all fall on top of him. And stay there until the starter trolley rolls into the bay. Horsfall is, of course, the last to get to his feet: he looks as if he has enjoyed himself thoroughly. Dunn grabs his forage cap from him and we climb aboard.

At 1,000 feet, Vernon is still climbing. I remind him that the bombing exercise is to be from this height, but he replies that the $H_2S$ one is to be from 5,000. To which I retort: 'I know, I know, but we're briefed to do the bombing ex. first.' This he ignores and continues climbing. At 5,000ft. he levels out and I start playing with the $H_2S$ getting the most beautiful of traces when over Scunthorpe (all those steelworks there). Pick up good traces over Hull then follow the banks of the Humber up to Grimsby, which comes up but faintly. Then I announce the $H_2S$ exercise to be over and that I wish to have a shot at flying the thing.

Vernon says over his dead body, but I remind him that I am a failed pilot, having been kicked out of No. 4 British Flying Training School in Phoenix, Arizona, in early 1942, and that I have about 10 hours solo to my credit in PT17As (a Stearman bi-plane trainer): also that I'm supposed to be 'Second Dickie' in the event of him being put out of action during an op. I put on what I fancy to be my most authoritative voice and bellow that I insist.

At which the screams start coming over the intercom begging Vernon not to give in: and Horsfall intimates his intention that, in the event of 'that Scots bastard' taking over, he's going to bale out.

But Vernon motions to Sgt. Griggs to vacate his Flight Engineer's seat beside him and to move aft. That done, Vernon locks the controls, rises, and motions me to occupy his pilot's seat. Once I've done that he unlocks again and the Lanc is mine. I fly straight and level for a while then do a gentle bank to port. Vernon taps me on the shoulder and points to the altimeter. I am losing height. I ease back on the control column and we're OK again. Vernon has plugged into the intercom and announces he's going to crawl into my bomb aimer's compartment 'just to see what it's like when airborne'.

Cries over the intercom: 'For Christ's sake don't leave him there on his own'; 'All those ops and now to buy it simply because of a daft haggis-basher'. Plus a sonorous rendering of The Lord's Prayer.

I tell Vernon not to touch anything in my compartment, otherwise we might be dropping practice bombs on some poor English village. He crawls into it, but is soon back. 'Right, you've had enough,' he says. 'I'll take over now.'

Sighs of relief over the intercom: and The Lord's Prayer terminates.

Once Vernon is back at the controls, we suddenly remember about the bombing exercise.He asks for a course for the Bombing Range and, once on it, starts losing height until we're at 1,000 feet. We come across the range so quickly that I'm not all that happy with the run-in. So I tell Vernon to go round again. Which gives rise to dark mutterings over the intercom about the inefficiency, the idiocy – indeed, the complete cluelessness – of bods who're *supposed* to be bomb aimers. But I have it bang-on that second time and have the satisfaction of seeing my practice bombs straddle the target quite perfectly.

On our return we have, of course, to report to Sandy Mansfield, the Bombing Leader. He asks what took us so long? We reply that we spent more time than we had intended on the $H_2S$ exercise. 'Had to get it just right,' I amplify. To which Sandy gives a disbelieving snort.

'Anyway,' he adds, 'you got direct hits on the target. Quite immaculate bombing, if I may say so.'

'Probably some other bloody Lanc's bombing,' grunts Horsfall. 'In fact, I'm certain of it.'

'Oh no,' says Sandy, 'it was you OK. The bombing range chappies got your number – you went round twice, remember – and their time-on-range coincides with yours shown here.' He nods at our log. 'Oh yes, it certainly was you who did that excellent piece of bombing.'

'Of course it was,' I nod affably.

'Only one little criticism, though,' continues Sandy. 'Such a little thing, it's scarcely worth mentioning.'

'And that is?' I am still smiling.

'Merely,' says Sandy, now also smiling, 'You bombed the wrong f . . . . . g range.'

**31 July 1944**

A Flying Officer – he has been at Wickenby for only a short while and I don't have his name – is a very keen horseman and already has become very pally with a local farmer who is also keen on horses. As a result, this F/O borrows a horse from his new-found friend on practically every occasion when he has a free hour or so. On his way to return the horse, if the bar is open, he tethers his stead outside the Mess and goes in for a quick pint. (Has, inevitably, earned himself the nickname of Hopalong Cassidy.)

Yesterday, he came into the ante-room just as the lunchtime bar opened. I was the only one there having gone in really just for cigarettes but, once there, deciding to stay for a pint. Hopalong (am pretty certain his name *is* Cassidy now that I come to think of it) ordered his pint. He demolished half of it in one mighty gulp, beamed broadly and announced to me that he had had one hell of a thirst, but that now he had slaked it he felt absolutely on top of the world. I could not resist it. I observed to him that maybe he had slaked his thirst and felt on top of the world, but what about his faithful nag out there which was so thirsty it was probably dying of it. Shaken when Hopalong admitted I had a point; he charged outside, untethered his horse and led it into the ante-room and up to the bar. He ordered a pint for it; also a basin. The steward produced both with an aplomb which suggested that an officer walking into his bar with a horse and ordering a pint and a basin was practically an everyday occurrence. Must say that the horse seemed to enjoy his pint. So much so that I bought him another. This produced from Hopalong the mild suggestion that I was trying to get his horse tight for some nefarious purpose known only to myself. I refuted this by saying I'd never been on a horse in my life and had no intention of – if no hand-brake on it I didn't want to know. The horse entered into this non-acrimonious exchange by demonstrating that, whatever training it might have had, Officers' Mess behaviour was not included in the itinerary. At which moment the Mess Secretary decided to look into the ante-room. To his question: 'What in the name of God is this?' I answered that it was a horse. He retorted that he knew a horse when he saw one, but – he glanced at the mound on the carpet – '*what* is this?'

There is in the RAF, and indeed all over the English-speaking world, a four letter noun most often used in this field, but Hopalong preferred the polite: 'manure'. At which the Mess Secretary referred to the little plot of ground outside his billet where he was growing some vegetables and politely invited us to convey the 'manure' from the Mess carpet to it. 'Yourselves,' he added threateningly, 'not my Mess staff – I'm not having them cleaning it up.'

Which we did. After, of course, first removing the horse. Smartly; before the effect of his two pints of beer manifested itself.

Halifax out in one of the bays has brought with it a rumour that we are to convert to that aircraft, which I reckon to be a load of rubbish. To convert from a superior aircraft like the Lanc to the Halibag! Just not on. Not that we look down on the Halibag: it's an excellent bomber. But not as excellent as the Lanc. (Reckon the Halibag boys would dispute that statement rather fiercely; they are as loyal to their aircraft as we are to ours.) In this connection one character in 12 Squadron who has flown operationally on Halifaxes as well as Lancs maintains that if you were well and truly bashed by flak or cannon and the aircraft broke up you'd be better off in a

Halibag than a Lanc because the former breaks into large sections which gives the crew a better chance of getting out by parachute. Even so, I'll stick to the Lanc!

From time to time we see Halifaxes on our ops. Usually in day time but occasionally at night too. The general public seem to think that virtually all heavy bombing is done by Lancs and tend to ignore the fact that Halifaxes are out in force also. One thing about the Halifax that I certainly don't go for and that is that the exhausts are clearly visible at night and thus act as a magnet to the night fighters. Some attribute high Halifax losses on night ops to this. Believe tests were made with anti-glow shrouds secured over the exhaust stubs but that these affected performance and ease of handling quite seriously. Vernon says the Halibag isn't easy to handle anyway but as far as I know he's never flown one so maybe he's not quite accurate.

Anyway, glad I wasn't on Halifaxes for that Peenemunde raid in August of last year. (Peenemunde is some German experimental station about 120 miles north of Berlin.) Each Halifax, for the 1,300 miles there and back, carried a bomb load of 5,500lbs. They seemed to have been attacked by JU88s from the island of Sylt and from there on by ME110s and FW190s. While the attack was reported as being successful, 40 aircraft were lost. A lot of the chaps, that.

All the Halifaxes seem to be based in Yorkshire with the odd base here in Lincolnshire. Met a Halifax bomb aimer who had been along with us on the Stuttgart prang of 24/25 July. He had it pretty rough having two engines shot out of the thing (maybe not exactly shot out but certainly put out of action). Somehow or another they got back on two. Said it was his final op and thank Christ for that. He also said it had always been his intention, if hit about the eyes by flak or cannon, that rather than spend the rest of his life blind, he'd simply dive out of his escape hatch and drop down to a quick death. I couldn't agree with him over that: I mean, you could be hit across the face and *think* you were blinded but in the event not be. No, I wouldn't do that. Still, a terrible thought to be blinded for life. All these beautiful things you'd no longer be able to see. Doesn't bear thinking about: want to forget it.

| | |
|---|---|
| *Op. No. 24* | *31 July–1 August 1944* |
| *Target* | Secret installations (rockets) at NIEPPE |
| *A/C 'B'* | *Load* 18 x 500lbs. |
| *Take off* | 20:00hrs. *Duration* 3.05hrs. |
| *Height* | 11,000ft. |
| *Flak* | Light but concentrated |
| *S/Ls* | Nil |
| *E/A* | None sighted |

Bombed on red Target Indicators through light cloud. Bombing seemed quite well concentrated.

So it's rockets now as well as those robot-bombs. Must be worried to take us off Germany to bomb secret installations such as these. Odd how yesterday we were so reconciled to our remaining efforts being over the Reich only to find ourselves with a soft target like this for very next one.

Owing to base being U/S due to low cloud and ground mists, we were diverted to Worksop. No beds – had to simply lie around in the Mess waiting for weather to clear. Returned to Squadron at 14.40hrs. today (1 August).

**Note (of distinction!)**
Won the Peeing Competition before this effort. Urinating on a flight presents something of a problem, so, just before we get in and start up the Merlins, we form a line outside the Lanc in order to empty our bladders. The one who can pee the farthest is, naturally, the winner. Also, naturally, no prizes. I went the furthest this time: helped, I'd think, by the fact that I'd had a thirst and had drunk about a pint of water; also by the fact that I'd knocked back my can of orange juice. Anyway, I won.

Quite a sight, I'm sure, to see a crew of seven all lined up having a widdle and making a competition out of it. A hysterical sight, I think, to a WAAF who passed by on her bike in the middle of the proceedings and giggling like mad. Well, it isn't every day a girl sees seven penises all at the same time, especially seven ejecting competitive parabolas.

On one occasion this ritual – for that is what it has become – was supervised, unasked, by a sergeant armourer. Also unasked, he pronounced that Vernon had the biggest and I had the smallest, commentating at the same time how odd it was that smallish guys had big ones and tallish guys had small ones. I informed him that it wasn't the *size* of a weapon that mattered, that it really was the manner in which it was deployed, but I think this was rather over his head. This scintillating conversation went on quite a bit with Horsfall adding, somewhat illogically, that if he could have managed an erection he could have out-pissed us all. An erection! Here out in the aircraft bay and about to take off on a bombing mission which could mean the end of us! Don't think I could have accomplished that even if Betty Grable and Lana Turner, both nude, had appeared to wish us a safe journey with the promise of erotic delights on our return.

**1 August 1944**

Continuing on the fascinating subject chronicled at the foot of the Nieppe effort; before that op we were airborne at 12:00 on a bombing exercise at 1,000 feet coupled with some $H_2S$ practice. (Returned at back of 14:00hrs. and airborne again at 20:00hrs.)

It was during this exercise – in 'B' – that, while lying in the bomb aimer's position, I felt something wet dripping on to me. I said to Vernon that there must be a leak in the nose somewhere above me. Vernon asked if the fact that he was having a pee couldn't have anything to do with this, could it? I looked up and immediately shouted at him to put it away, that he was drowning me. Laughter from all the rest plus advice to sue him. For, beside the pilot there is a funnel from which runs a pipe down from the side of his seat, across the top of the bomb aimer's compartment, and out on the starboard side. (Why on earth it can't avoid the bomb aimer's compartment and make its exit on the *port* side defeats me.) This pipe had developed a fault and the wetness dropping on me was Vernon's urine. Vernon said sorry, that he was finished anyway. To which I replied that at least I was the only one of them who could honestly and truthfully say he had been pissed upon from a great height. Horsfall said you couldn't call 1,000 feet a great height, but didn't reply when I retorted that it was when compared to standing at a urinal.

Funny how the bodily functions under circumstances other than the normal excite the interest of so many people – especially civilians. My stepfather, for instance, wondered how I relieved myself on a long flight, of say, 6 or 7 hours. I told him that I tried to avoid consuming much liquid before a flight and that I always had a 'last one' out in the parking bay before climbing aboard. but he was very keen on an answer so I explained to him how, if the call became too pressing, I simply opened the hatch to my right – normally used for ejecting propaganda leaflets or window – and used that. I added that the slipstream unfailingly returned most of it to where it had originated, which he thought very funny.

(God, it's becoming difficult to get away from this subject! But I might as well complete it now I've started . . . )

Others ask outright what you do if you have an urgent need to defecate. I tell them that if you're on the other side of the Channel, or even half-way back across the North Sea, you just forget it. If they persist I tell them to use their imagination!

Actually, we do have an Elsan chemical toilet aboard. It's near the tail, just forward of the rear turret. Naturally, very securely clamped down. It could be used if you were suddenly caught short on a training flight.

None of us has ever used it. That's for certain, because were you desperate to avail yourself of the facilities it offered, you'd have to seek Vernon's permission to leave your position, a request which all of us would hear: next you'd have to pull out your intercom lead, make your slow, stumbling way along the catwalk (unless you were the rear-gunner) to the Elsan, plug your intercom lead into the socket beside it and inform Vernon you'd arrived: next, removal of your parachute harness coupled, perhaps, with the removal of certain parts of flying clothing together with that beneath: lastly, a wrestling match to remove the security clamps from the lid. And by the time you'd got through that little drill if your need had been so dreadfully urgent you'd be too late. Far too late . . .

Our training flight on 31 July took us near Liverpool. Which reminded me of the day in early June of last year when the Louis Pasteur docked there after its voyage from Canada. Don't know how many thousands of returning RAF personnel, Canadians and Americans were on board, but that ship was certainly crammed.

How filthy, how scruffy, how miserable the docks at Liverpool seemed after the clean freshness of New Brunswick: one heard the Canadians and Yanks expressing their dismay at their first sight of England.

All even more dismayed when informed delay in docking due to dockers' strike. Really, could hardly believe this. Dockers on strike in the middle of a war? Yet evidently it was true. Wondered what would happen if the dockers at Hamburg went on strike.

After another day we docked. A great number of us had stocked our trunks, cases and kitbags with items unobtainable in the UK. Things like nylons (which the girls here had heard about but had never possessed – unless over-pally with Yanks) razor blades, cigarette lighters, tinned fruits, cigars, tins of meat, etc: and, of course, hundreds of cigarettes. When a crane conveying a large netful of luggage from ship to shore suddenly tipped the net so that twenty of thirty cases and trunks fell from it into the water, the scream of anger which rose from the Pasteur might have been heard on the other side of the Atlantic. The scream was accompanied by a barrage of coins aimed at the dockers. I too threw coins firmly believing I'd seen my green trunk among those deposited into the Mersey. Some of the dockers were badly cut about the face. Maybe it wasn't fair to throw coins as we did (after all, it could have been a genuine accident) but I think most felt that it was the result of a couldn't-care-less attitude; and that, anyway, the bastards had just been on strike, hadn't they?

So it wasn't a very enjoyable reintroduction to England. The journey hadn't been all that enjoyable either: crammed together far too tightly for that: and the Pasteur, being provisioned by the Americans, was OK for fags, ice cream, coke, chewing gum, candy bars, etc., but was dry; you couldn't even buy yourself a bottle of beer aboard her.

Different going the other way. Refrigerator ship returning to America for supplies and carrying twenty aircrew on their way for training. British provisioned, so poor food but plenty of booze. Two gramophones supplied to us (same stock of HMV records for each!) Most played was Harry Roy's 'Amapola'.

An over-zealous Physical Training Instructor after a struggle managed to get us on to the deck to play a silly game with three big rubber balls. When all three, as a result of quite excellent co-ordination on our part, went overboard simultaneously and a grumbling captain had to detail someone with a rifle to sink them, we saw the last of such silly and entirely unnecessary exertions. Also saw the last of that particular PTI.

**Entered some days later**

That diversion to Worksop after Nieppe was really quite a bind. We landed there at about 23:15hrs. and it was past midnight by the time we arrived at the Mess. There, we were rather grudgingly accepted. No, sorry we couldn't give you a meal; you see, all the cooks are now off-duty and long since a-bed and we couldn't possibly expect them to get up and prepare you a meal, could we? We said, well, we hadn't eaten since early evening, having taken off at 20:00hrs., and were literally starving. This produced, still rather grudgingly, some sandwiches – of that truly wretched Spam – and coffee which we wouldn't have recognised as such had they not acquainted us of the doubtful fact. Then into the ante-room (no blankets or such-like) to get through what remained of the night. Much bad language all round.

At least we got breakfast out of them at 08:00. No fresh eggs, of course; that dreadful powdered stuff which I simply cannot get down. Managed about three slices of toast (on marge) and two cups of tea. We also got lunch from them and that too was a meal I do not wish to remember.

Writing this, it seems ungracious to be moaning away about getting poor food and having to spend the night sprawling in an easy-chair while, just across the Channel, our forces, probably soaking, cold and dirty, eating iron rations when they can, would consider us to be living in the lap of luxury. Also, we are in no danger, while they are. Yes, indeed it is ungracious: very much so.

**Later still**

Laugh of the week. We each get a Mess Bill from the Mess at Worksop. (Certainly on the ball in *that* respect.) It's for 5/6d and itemises 'evening coffee', 'breakfast', 'lunch' and, of all things, 'overnight accommodation'! We have to pay it, of course. And, strictly speaking, we should receive a rebate from our own Mess for not having enjoyed these items at Wickenby. But things don't work out that way. Can't get over it, though – 5/6d for *that* . . .

| | |
|---|---|
| *Op. No. 25* | *2 August 1944* |
| *Target* | Secret installations (rocket-bombs?) at LES CATELLIER |
| *A/C 'B'* | *Load* 11 x 400lbs.<br>4 x 500lbs. |
| *Take off* | 15:40hrs. *Duration* 3.40hrs. |
| *Height* | 18,000ft. |
| *Flak* | Light enough but predicted. Seemed heavier guns than usual. We were hit on the run up: later I counted at least twenty holes in the kite – one in port wing, rest in tailplane and rudders. Some of the holes were pretty big at that |
| *E/A* | None sighted |

New tactics on this daylight op. We flew in formation led by two Mosquitos and dropped our bombs when they dropped theirs. But the cloud had cleared when we got to the target so we would have been much more accurate had we bombed visually. Would have preferred that in any case.

We had a passenger on this one. A trick cyclist from Group. He had come, we were informed, to record what was called 'the behavioural pattern' of a seasoned, operational aircrew. A W/C but, of course, wingless, otherwise we wouldn't have behaved as we did. Sounds a bit childish, I suppose, as I sit here after the op writing it up, but, well, we did it. And I suppose I must take the blame because I started it when we got out of the 'bus alongside the Lanc. I started biting at my lower lip and nervously informed Vernon that I wasn't going. Vernon entered into the spirit of the thing and said if I didn't get into the kite there and then it would be a Court Martial. To which I replied that maybe he was skipper but I was senior to him. At which we squared up to each other. Horsfall came into the act at that point by saying he felt sick and managing to do a bloody good impression of throwing up. And so on. All of which the trick cyclist noted.

And our language deteriorated even more, if that be possible, virtually every second word being 'fucking'. Then, when inland from the French coast and some rather accurate flak burst near us peppering the fuselage with shrapnel, there were screams and shouts over the intercom – 'turn back', 'Mummy', 'I don't want to die', plus a not inconsiderable selection of blasphemies. Really, it was most unfair to the chap who was just trying to do his job. (He didn't look very happy with the flak, but one couldn't have expected him to be.)

**PS (written on 7 August)**

Today we were summond to the Squadron Commander's office. Winco Nelson was seated at his desk, his hat on and looking very formal. We entered and saluted. He said to get out, to come in again and to salute *properly* this time. Which we did. He then looked evenly at each of us in turn after which he picked up some papers from his desk. 'This,' he intoned 'is the Group Psychiatrist's report on you as a crew during the Les Catellier op.' He shook his head slowly from side to side. 'Really, what a shower you are. Consider yourselves reprimanded. Now get out!'

We did. His laughter caught up with us while we were still in the corridor.

**2 August 1944**

'Phoned Ann, then my folks. Usually do that after a heavy raid on Germany has been reported by BBC. They hear about it, and the losses, and immediately wonder whether you were involved: and, more importantly, whether you got back safely. So I try to 'phone quite often. Naturally, you can't tell them if you were on ops the previous night, far less the target: RAF wouldn't like you doing that on the, admittedly slight, chance that somehow or another the Germans might, as a result of your indiscretion, learn that the Lancs which bombed somewhere or another were based on Wickenby. Don't know what they would, or could, do about it if they did, but that's the RAF's attitude. So, after saying you're fit and well, you chat about the weather, hear the latest about local friends, or relatives, join in a gentle moan about the latest reduction in the meat, or sugar, or whatever ration (though such things pass us by here at Wickenby where, while I suppose we must be on rations of some kind, one wouldn't think so by the standard of our messing where the quantity is matched by the quality). Usually a question about the possibility of leave to which I have to reply no chance, we're too busy (which is about as far as I can hint).

Sometimes my mother asks for the Wickenby 'phone number, but I always tell her it's secret. Don't want her 'phoning here, on an impulse, to find out whether I'm OK, not being able to contact me and, as a result, panicking.

With conversation beginning to flag, maybe a reference to a recently seen film. Sometimes, with my folk, I've got to tell them somebody else is waiting to use the 'phone as an excuse to ring off. Can only use that one occasionally, though.

So often feel slightly depressed after 'phoning. Suppose it's because Ann and my folk are living in a world so different to mine. Or, more likely, because it is I who am living in a world different to theirs. At times what I'm engaging in here at Wickenby all seems like a dream. Not exactly the most pleasant of dreams, but not a nightmare. No, certainly not that.

| | |
|---|---|
| *Op. No. 26* | *3 August 1944* |
| *Target* | Caves containing rocket-bomb stores at TROSSY ST. MAXIMIN |
| *A/C 'D'* | *Load* 11 x 1,000lbs.<br>4 x 500lbs. |
| *Take off* | 11:30hrs. *Duration* 4.45hrs. |
| *Flak* | Heavy predicted stuff. Hit again in port inner which had to be feathered – consequently I had to put manual settings on my bomb sight. Also hit in port wing (several ugly, big holes) and in fuselage several times. WOP slightly injured. This heavy flak really shook each and every one of us: in a way it was worse that the stuff they shove up over the Reich. And, of course, it's coming at you in day-light. Don't like flak at any time but it seems nastier by day |
| *E/A* | None. No wonder with all those Spits milling around the sunny, summer sky desperate for a fight |

We had to fly in 'D' as 'B' is still being repaired. Now we've made such a mess of 'D' that she too will be unserviceable for a day or two.

Butch Harris must be more cheesed off than ever with so many of his beloved Lancs still being taken off the task of flattening Germany and diverted to bombing places like rocket sites, secret installations, railway yards and such-like. Still, as far as we are concerned there are no complaints!

Sandy Mansfield, our Bombing Leader, invited me into his office today. Went completely on my guard when he informed me that I was just about the most accurate bomb aimer in the Squadron. Which was simply his preface to inviting me to go on a Bombing Leader's course. Naturally, he added, that meant promotion. I said no dice. For two reasons. The first was that it meant leaving the crew who'd find themselves with a new bomb aimer for their last four. The second was that you don't get off those last four: as Bombing Leader you still have to slip them in, but it's usually (though not always) with a sprog crew whose bomb aimer has reported sick or has been wounded. No way I was going to risk these last four with a new, inexperienced crew. To be honest with myself, the second reason was the main one.

Heard later that Horsfall had been offered a Gunnery Leader's course, but that he too had turned it down. Probably for the same reasons. Glad he did so. I don't think any of us would have been happy with a strange, and perhaps inexperienced, gunner in that mid-upper turret. He didn't tell me about it and I didn't tell him – or, for that matter, anybody else.

**3 August 1944**

Nowadays we regard ourselves as very experienced operational types, today's effort over Trossy St. Maximin being our 26th op, which makes us (and it is 'us' not me only, Vernon and Horsfall having the same outlook) feel sorry for the sprog crews who, almost daily, arrive as replacements posted either to 12 or 626 Squadrons. They don't know, and can't be expected to know, a thing about operational flying: nothing, that is, other than what they've been told while under training. For them, as it was for us, it's the pay-off to that romantic, oh it's terrific to be prancing around with your flying brevet and your sergeant's tapes, or your Warrant Officer's crowns, or your Pilot Officer's or Flying Officer's rings, yes, I'm a hero and the girls are all a flutter and life's just absolutely bloody wonderful, I could keep on going for ever and ever with a life like this. But the word 'life' when you crawl into your pit is the one which jerks you right back into the 'this is it' league. For you that is just what is going to be forfeit. Unless you amass 'luck' in quantities so large you'd never believe it. Which, so far, we as a crew have what with all those comparatively easy French trips and so few over Germany.

But back to the fresh crews. They ask the inevitable: (a) How many have you done? (b) What's it like? (c) Do you get scared when the night fighters trail you? To which we answer: (a) the truth, (b) f . . . . . g awful, (c) yes, with the word 'shitless' added. Which is not very fair, really. But it's us only a short couple of months ago, isn't it? When, just like them, absolutely green and scared, wondering what we've done to get ourselves in a situation like this, we arrived here at Wickenby: and later finding you've got the oldest, clapped-out Lancasters on the unit – you don't get a top-notch job until you've proved you've got a reasonable chance of not losing it the very first time you take the thing abroad – and you get around to wishing you simply had not joined.

Yes, we feel sorry for them. And on the whole don't do very much to make life easier for them. Maybe they'll not make it, less likely they will. If the latter, then it'll be their turn to feel sorry for the following lots of newcomers. And by then either, and nearing the end of our tour at that, we ourselves will have bought it: or, with luck, will have completed it safely and, I am sure, will be behaving unbearably off-hand towards any air-crew who haven't been on ops. As for the Army, we'll continue our present practice of referring to them as 'brown jobs' and wondering out loud what they spend their time doing. And as for the Navy, we'll keep on assuring them, as we never fail to do, that we're most grateful to them for convoying all that petrol to our shores so that we in our Lancs can get on with winning the war for them.

No wonder we're not all that popular with the rest of the Services! It's just as well most don't take us all that seriously. Most: the odd bod does. Which now and then gives rise to a certain amount of unbrotherly love. This, however, usually is diminished over a couple of pints during the sinking of which our brothers-in-arms begin to conclude that, while our sense of humour is maybe not in line with theirs, the reason behind it all, in their opinion, is that air-crew who have done a tour of ops are invariably 'flak happy'.

After three or four pints, nearly all often become united in criticism of the Americans – most of it unfounded and most of it unfair.

But all that's in the future. If there's to be one.

**4 August 1944**

A brown job in the Mess. Not a young Army type in roughly the same age bracket as us, but a really ancient character. Had a moustache which reminded one of Kitchener. Maybe he wasn't truly Army; could have been, for all I knew, Lord Lieutenant of Lincolnshire or somewhere. But he reminded me so clearly of the ex-army pensioners who, at the beginning of the war, the RAF shoved into blue uniform and called them members of Aircrew Selection Boards.

They had such a Board in Edinburgh. At the Music Hall in George Street. And, indeed, the Music Hall was the most appropriate place for them. No idea whatever. I had volunteered for aircrew and had presented myself to them. Those ancient warriors had the knack of putting your back up the minute you entered their presence. Why did you want to volunteer for aircrew? for starters. There's only one answer to the question and it's not that which first springs to mind. Then, did I ride? There's an answer to that one too, but you dare not give it. Third, was I much good with a yacht? No answer to that daftie.

In short, I commended myself to them just as much as they commended themselves to me. One old boy suggested I go downstairs and enlist for a course leading to fitter or mechanic. I went downstairs all right. But not to enlist for a training course. I joined up as an aircraft *hand.* That was even lower down the scale than aircraft *man.* Two nice jobs for you if you're ac/h: one was general oddsbody (which was probably lavatory cleaner) and the other was ground gunner. Two weeks later I was called up as ground gunner.

Yes, this ancient brown job reminded me of that Board in late 1939 (or early 1940). Learned later that the RAF didn't waste much time in clearing them out.

Received a salute from a WAAF whose face I seemed to know.

So stopped and chatted with her. She'd been at Bawdsey at the same time as I had. We reminisced for quite a while on that delightful radar (known as RDF then) unit in Suffolk. She prefers here though: Bawdsey was too remote and also nothing much really happened there. She's an RT operator and finds it exciting being on an operational unit: would dearly like to be taken up in a Lanc, but so far hasn't managed it. She hinted that I might be able to fix this for her, but I had to be honest and say that this was beyond my powers. She's engaged to a sergeant air-gunner in 626 Squadron and worries every time he's on ops. Says they'd get married here and now if it wasn't for the fact that if they did it would mean her immediate posting away from Wickenby as the RAF won't allow husband and wife to serve on the same station. I didn't know such a rule applied, but it sounds sensible enough. She then switched on to the subject of discipline and started criticising her Section Officer who, she complained, was far too strict on all her girls. Obviously I couldn't take part in any discussion on this subject. It would have been, in RAF jargon, 'prejudicial to the maintenance of good discipline', so I made an excuse to break off the conversation.

Bawdsey! Think that was where I moved from boy to man. All in that hut were aircraft*hands* – not aircraft*men*: no trades, no skills, some of them pretty rough, some of them also pretty tough: took me all my time to hold my own with them. God, I was green! Learned a lot there: for example, if your bayonet scabbard went missing, you simply took someone else's: if your cap-badge disappeared you waited until someone left their forage cap lying around and took the badge from that. But you could leave your *personal* possessions lying around and nobody would help themselves to any of them. The NCO in charge of us was a Cpl. Walsh, called Curly. A regular who, because of the war, had received his two tapes much earlier than he would have in peace-time. Rather a surly character and not all that popular with us. He used to return to the billet at nights having spent quite a while in the NAAFI, shout 'ah, me effing pit', take a short run and fling himself on it. One evening we disconnected the hooks holding the bed springs, carefully putting back the three biscuits on top. Curly in due course entered, made his usual fond remark concerning his place of rest, his usual run, his usual dive on to it. The bed collapsed. Curly knocked himself out. Curly was not pleased.

But this business regarding moving from boy to man – it was Curly who accomplished it for me. Something he said, I think: about me being a haggis bashing bastard. I hit him one. As hard as I could. I might as well have hit a brick wall; he didn't even flinch. Now it's a terrible thing for an airman to hit an NCO. Court martial then glass-house. Wave goodbye to all thoughts of aircrew. Disaster at its worst. But Curly didn't do what he should have done. That is, put me on a charge. Instead, he took me to the gym, produced two pairs of boxing gloves. I thought well, he's heavy and lumbering; I'm light, so I'll dance all around him. Which I did. But any blows of mine which landed on him he simply brushed aside. He hit me once, which put me on my back. A second hit likewise. I felt that what I fondly regarded as my good looks were about to go for a Burton and packed it in. Cowardly? Of course it was!

But after that I was the only one in that billet on whom Curly bestowed a benevolent glance. Lying on top of my pit the next evening and Curly comes in and asks why am I not up at the NAAFI. Say I don't feel like going up to the effing NAAFI. Curly says it's because I'm effing well skint. I say I'm not. He glares that I am. Then he says 'Up to the effing NAAFI; that's an effing order, airman.' So I go. He buys me two pints. Notices that I'm not smoking so next 20 Woodbines. Then he tells me he kind of likes me. Which immediately puts me on the defensive. But no nonsense: the poor guy is absolutely devoid of friends – he simply wants somebody to speak to. He tells me about his younger days. Honestly, I've been so shielded that I didn't know how rough, how tough, life could be in a mining village in Yorkshire in the 1930s. Heavens, what you learn through joining the RAF; and how you mature.

When I left Bawdsey to go on my aircrew training Curly saw me off. Said he was glad to be effing well rid of an effing haggis bashing bastard like me and wished he'd put me on an effing charge for taking an effing poke at him. In which case he'd be seeing me off to the effing glasshouse instead of to aircrew training which, he explained, would have given him immeasurable pleasure. Only he didn't use the word 'immeasurable': he intoned that it would have given him 'much effing joy'.

Yes, fond memories of Curly. All brought back by meeting here at Wickenby that airwoman who'd served there. Wonder how Curly would react were I, all dolled up with bomb aimer's brevet and F/O rings, to bump into him. I suppose he would salute me. Then I would take him into the nearest boozer where all this business about drinking with 'other ranks' would be forgotten. Think probably it would end up with both of us being flung out.

**4 August 1944**

Have flung out my sergeant's tapes and the white armband. No point in holding on to these here at Wickenby even though they are reminders of a very pleasant time. When awarded our brevets in Canada we were paraded as sergeants. Those of us commissioned were informed of this the next day, told to remove our tapes and to wear a white band on the right arm to denote an officer awaiting his tailor's pleasure. But sporting sergeant's tapes was better fun than wearing a white band so I kept them up. Even stayed on in the

Sergeants' Mess at Mountainview. Visited a tailor and explained that my clothing allowance had not yet been paid. He couldn't have cared less and measured me there and then for my uniform. Eventually turned out of Sergeants' Mess: could hardly wear sergeant's stripes in the Officers' Mess so unstitched them and put on the white armband. Two weeks later a letter from the tailor. So downtown to get my uniform with the thin black and blue ring round each sleeve. With some trepidation warily watched first airman to approach me. I returned his salute then, remembering, called him back, told the surprised bod that his salute to me was my first as an officer and, accordingly, would he please accept this buck and thus preserve an old tradition. Sure he thought I was nuts, but took the dollar all the same. Don't know if it really is tradition (in Canada) to slip a buck to the first airman to salute you: probably just something that got about.

Seems a hundred years ago, that – not just about 18 months.

**Later**

Two things in the paper to chuckle over.

The first is that morality squads are to be formed to deal with girls who are 'soldier mad'. (If they confine their madness to the Army why should *we* in the RAF bother!) These are girls, so the paper says, who have gone astray, the problem being caused by lack of parental control, the glamour of uniforms, drink, and loneliness caused by the transfer of so many young women to factories long distances from their homes. Frankly, I don't see what these so-called morality squads can do to stop birds being 'soldier mad' if they want to. 'Goodie goodies' behind it all, I reckon. Can't stand those types.

The other – on the same page – is that Hitler has got himself a popsie. According to this report from Sweden he is so obsessed with her that he's even neglecting affairs of State. Her name is Eva Braun. The report concludes by quoting from a 'usually reliable source' that the Führer's fascination for the dame is so great that he is showing signs of personal deterioration. Show it to Vernon who grins and says it's probably because Adolf's dipping his wick far too much; and that, anyway, if the bugger quickly f . . . . . d himself to death the war would suddenly be over and we wouldn't have to complete our tour.

**4 August 1944**

Mess games under way again tonight. Kicked off with the pyramid effort in which three of four bods crouch down and press their shoulders against the wall at the same time encircling each other with their arms. Rather like one half of a rugby scrum. Then those remaining take running jumps from the far end of the ante-room and try to build on this base. Success is proclaimed if the pyramid can be added to until the last to jump on to it has his back against the ceiling. Alas, this stage was not reached tonight as some ill-intentioned individuals tickled the testicles of the centre members of the base. Which caused the entire structure to collapse amid much shouting and not a little swearing. All was not lost, however, because the struggling mob on the floor involved itself into two rugger teams. It wasn't a question of pilots and navigators versus bomb aimers and gunners: it was more a question of everybody against everybody: with, it goes without saying, Horsfall playing a most prominent part. The damage was not all that extensive; just two chairs demolished. On the personal side, Vernon got his blouse ripped, Horsfall lost his tie and I got a slight tear in my trousers (not my best ones, I'm glad to record).

After a rest, three started on the old footsteps-up-the-wall-and-across-the-ceiling nonsense. Just after the ante-room had been redecorated too; the Mess Secretary will do his flaming nut. That done, two started on: 'Cats on the rooftops, cats on the tiles, cats with (a certain part of their anatomy) wreathed in smiles', but this tailed off when nobody else seemed to want to listen and either went off to play billiards, cards or dominoes. Some even returned to the bar. One sat himself in an easy chair to read *The Times*, but hastily put it down again when he spotted a crafty and cunning advance being made on him with a lighted match. A Flying Officer from Accounts suddenly came into the ante-room and very politely asked if we objected to his playing a record on the radiogram (a rather elegant HMV model). In a somewhat condescending manner, one of us indicated that he might. The guy put on: 'Pomp and Circumstance' at full blast. This had a dampening effect on the discussion now taking place at the bar. No need to elaborate on that discussion except to observe that its subject material would not have been acceptable in a Church Hall back in Edinburgh: nor, indeed, in a Church Hall anywhere. The discussion survived the record: but when the Accounts chap followed with Richard Tauber bellowing out: 'Heart's delight', he was told to turn it down a bit. For good measure he was informed that, anyway, we would all prefer to listen to Miller, Dorsey, Shaw and the like. Taking the hint, he reduced the volume and at the end of the record took off. The discussion continued without everybody having to shout their opinion: or, in some cases, relate their experiences. But eventually even those who had been the most enthusiastic when it was launched began to lose interest in the discussion which then ground to a halt. People began to drift off to their billets. When I left there was only one bod at the bar and even he said it was his last. For that evening, he was quick to add.

| | |
|---|---|
| *Op. No. 27* | *5 August 1944* |
| *Target* | Oil storage depots at BLAYE (NR. BORDEAUX) |
| *A/C 'A'* | *Load* 9 x 1,000lbs.<br>3 x 500lbs. |
| *Take off* | 14:10hrs. *Duration* 8.25hrs. |
| *Height* | Nought feet until near target: bombing height 8,500ft. |
| *Flak* | Nil |
| *E/A* | None around |

Another daylight op. And still I don't like them. Flew at sea-level due West then turned into Bay of Biscay still at nought feet (all this so as to escape German radar). Passed over a couple of fishing boats and exchanged waves. A Lanc flying on our starboard side suddenly dived into the water. I could hardly believe what I was seeing – one second he was there, next second he was under. Nobody else in crew saw it. Noted in my log to report at Interrogation. Climbed to 8,500 to bomb. Unfortunately, electrics for the bomb doors failed (probably all that sea spray) so couldn't release my bombs. Brought them back. Weather clamped at base so diverted to Church Broughton: returned to base at 15:00hrs. the following day.

The entire effort one long bore: especially going all that way and not being able to bomb these oil storage tanks. There they were and we couldn't get at them.

I hope 'B' for Baker all repaired now: don't like flying in any other kite.

We have been told (orally!) to take the French letters off our guns. Owing to shortage of armourers an Order had come out saying all gunners and bomb aimers had to service their own guns after an op. OK if you've fired your guns, but not if you haven't. So, in order to keep the moisture from the barrels when flying, we pulled French letters over the muzzles and thus saved ourselves some effort. Next, about half the Squadron was taking off with eight condoms hanging from the 303s much to the amusement of the WAAFs. Not to the amusement of a visiting Group Captain, however, so off they came. (They say we are to be issued with round perspex caps to fit over the muzzles: I think this is purely coincidental and in no way connected with our 'illegal' use of contraceptives . . .)

**Entered some days later**
These diversions because of duff weather at Wickenby are a bind.

This one to Church Broughton should be recorded, however, as our 'treatment' differed greatly to that accorded us at Worksop. Again, past midnight by the time we arrived at the Mess. But on this occasion a WAAF Sergeant-cook had volunteered (at least we were *informed* she had volunteered) to come in and prepare us a meal. Ham and eggs – fresh ones. Delightful. They said sorry, but no beds so we'd have to spend the rest of the night in the ante-room. They furnished us with blankets. No swearing this time; absolutely none whatsoever.

A good hearty breakfast at 08:00. An excellent lunch before we take off for base. All in such a good mood that Vernon says what about flying back at nought feet (strictly forbidden)? We all agree and I scramble down into the nose. Quite fascinating, really, roaring across the English country-side just above tree level, having to ease up over the hills, down into valleys, and so on. Probably scared the living daylights out of all sorts of people (who, even so, manage to wave to us). And I'm sure it doesn't do livestock below us any good. Still, a good time is had by all.

**Later still**

Yes, a Mess Bill from Church Broughton. For 3/6d this time. It itemises 'evening meal', 'breakfast' and 'lunch', but says nothing about 'overnight accommodation'. Don't grudge that 3/6d . . .

**6 August 1944**

A F/O navigator asked if he could borrow my Raleigh to go to Lincoln. Said he had a date with an ATS officer who he considered so much a cert that he'd already booked a hotel room. Said I'd be the last man to deny a bod his oats and agreed. Returned it the next afternoon. He wasn't all that full of joy; she'd gone with him to the hotel OK but once in the bedroom had burst into tears, said it would be the first time and she wanted to wait until she was married anyway. They slept in the same bed, each at the far side and no operational activities took place. He is not seeing her again: says if he's going to get the chop he wants to dip it a bit more before that happens. I said not around here he wouldn't. He replied that he didn't know about that and, referring obliquely to a WAAF in the Radio section, added that she was known to be of a generous nature.

Then, and only then, did he tell me he'd knackered the Sturmey-Archer 3 speed gear on my bike. I grinned at him that he shouldn't have vented his sexual frustration on my old Raleigh. He said it wasn't that – it had simply packed up. Offered to pay for it but I said it would probably have packed up with me anyway. Cost me thirty bob. How costs have risen; it cost only a guinea to install when new. Still, says a lot for British workmanship it lasting all that time especially despite all the rough treatment that Raleigh has been handed.

On the subject of my bike, it was the means of bumping into rather an attractive WAAF. Debatable whose fault it was, but it doesn't really matter. Anyway, we stood around for quite a while chatting. Her name is Donovan – not unsurprisingly known as 'Donnie' to her oppos – and she's a LACW RT operator on 12 Squadron. To her relief, her bike, which was a service issue, was undamaged. Odd how the RAF, nightly losing Lancs costing umpteen thousands each, guards its issue bikes as if they were worth millions: if you are lucky enough to get one you have to sign for it; and if you lose it – or, as is more likely, it's whipped – you have to fork up for the thing. (Unless you can whip somebody else's, that is.) Which, she said, was what had happened to her lamp: when going on duty she had padlocked her bike but had forgotten to take her lamp on duty with her. So much whipping of lamps there's such a shortage of them that it's quite usual for WAAF teleprinter operators, met assistants, RT operators, etc. all coming off duty together, and it being dark, to have only one lamp among, say, five or six. They then operate a kind of convoy system towards the WAAF site with the one girl possessing a lamp acting as Pathfinder and the rest cycling behind. On one such occasion she told me that there was a terrific crash at the rear of the convoy accompanied by much shouting and swearing. All hastily dismounted, calling for the WAAF with the lamp. The beam of this revealed an aircrew sergeant lying spreadeagled on the road. In the darkness away from the beam LACW Donovan picked up the NCO's forage cap. She found it sodden and for a dreadful moment thought that in the fall from his bike the bod must have split his head open. But as she held the headgear she became aware of the strong smell of beer: a sniff at it revealed it was soaking in the stuff. By now the NCO had regained his feet. He was as drunk as a lord. He lurched about trying to collect the remains of his bike, at the same time informing them it was the third occasion in the month he'd cycled into the back of a mob of lightless WAAFs. Then, draping the twisted mess round his neck, he staggered away into the night. Before doing so he intimated that he didn't go much on WAAFs, especially ones who giggled as much as they were doing. Only, as LACW Donovan said, he expressed this in rather stronger terms . . .

**6 August 1944**

Have referred occasionally to Wing Commander Nelson, the New Zealander who is OC No. 12 Squadron. Now there's a man I think everybody would follow practically anywhere. Quiet and unassuming (but am sure he could be a strict disciplinarian if anybody deliberately did anything which interfered with the efficient running of his Squadron). Comes into the Mess when we're having a pint: usually stands his hand but, to our delight, is not against having one on us. When things become boisterous he beats it: he's not going to be involved in any situation where he has to reprimand in the Mess any of his crews, no matter how lightly.

Then he's at every briefing. You just know he'd like to be coming with you. Understand that, as CO, he's not allowed to come on any op, no matter how comparatively safe it might sound. Also understand that, despite this injunction, he's flown on one or two lately when a pilot, at the very last moment, has called off sick (no doubt on the excuse that if he *hadn't* done so, the Lanc would have had to abort the operation: it wouldn't have washed with his superiors, though, had anything happened to him).

Winco Nelson is also there at de-briefing no matter the time of day or night. Tries to have a word with everybody: sounds melodramatic, but he conveys the impression that you are not 'Butch's' (or anybody else's, for that matter) aircrew – you are *his*.

**7 August 1944**

When we arrived here I commented favourably on the quality of the messing. So often I have found, as regards RAF catering, that first good impressions were not maintained in that the menus became repetitive and monotonous (eg. 'Ah, it's shepherd's pie – it must be Tuesday'); or that the quality fell away alarmingly, the sole cause perhaps being the posting elsewhere of the chief cook. But not here at Wickenby. The meals are varied, a great deal of imagination is used, they are attractively served and the quality is absolutely first class. When I reflect on what are in effect our rations and compare them with those of the civilians, I feel a bit piggish. Which, I suppose, is stupid.

On the subject of food, when I was last home my mother had hoarded her rations, plus those of my stepfather, in order to provide a good evening meal. She is an excellent cook, but despite that I had a job getting it down; fact is, I have become used to a lot better: and I've probably become somewhat fussy. Will soon change my tune if I'm ever shot down and end up in the bag . . .

Back to Wickenby; we are served by WAAFs most of whom are very attractive. They can't do enough for us. Some of the chaps try to cash in on this latter aspect and date them. The RAF do not like this at all. I remember, when first I was commissioned, being one of those given a little talk by a Squadron Leader who, in effect, said to us: 'You can't expect a WAAF to drop her knickers for you on the one evening and cock you up one the next morning.' But it goes further than that. If a WAAF becomes pregnant she is discharged from the Service and the RAF find it uncomfortable to the extreme if it comes out that the father is an RAF officer. Especially if it gets into the popular press. They fear the suggestion that fond mothers, in letting their daughters volunteer for the WAAF, are exposing their beloved ones to the tender mercies of sex-starved RAF officers all of whom are firmly convinced that the holding of the King's Commission also confers with it something akin to *droit de seigneur*. No, the RAF do not like this at all. Different with an airman: he puts a WAAF in the Club, she gets discharged and he gets posted.

On the joint subjects of rations and WAAFs, Sgt. Dunn maintains he's getting his rations from a popsie in the Parachute Section. But he harps on about this so often, and to so great a length, that we think it's merely wishful thinking. Funny, but those who talk about dipping it practically all over the place really seldom do. It's the ones who keep quiet about it who are the active ones in this field. And field it is – here there's nowhere else!

Still on the subject of WAAFs – and in no way connected with Sergeant Dunn's boasting above – met up again with LACW Donovan, the RT operator. Nearly fell off my bike with surprise. She was sitting in the back seat of the most dreadful wreck of an Austin Seven I have ever seen and beside her was a WAAF corporal. In the front a RN lieutenant was sitting beside the driver, a ground staff sergeant. The Austin Seven was travelling at, I'd say, about 5mph: which was no doubt attributable to the fact that one of the wheels was completely devoid of tyre. I dismounted and watched progress. The Austin stopped and I received the cheeriest of LACW waves. She got out. No salute – I think that would have embarrassed everybody around. She then introduced me. The WAAF corporal, whose name was Bunty and who worked in the Met Office, was the fiancée of the Sergeant and the navy type was her brother. They had been out celebrating (which was quite obvious). I nodded and murmured my congratulations. She replied that it wasn't the engagement they'd been celebrating – it was the trial run of the Austin Seven. At which I thought it would be diplomatic to get back on my bike and take off. But before I could do so she explained that Tony – he was the sergeant – was an engineer and that he'd discovered somewhere or another this wreck of a car. He'd picked it up for virtually nothing and had worked on it to make it road worthy. Deciding eventually that it was (though I think the police might not have come to the same decision) the four of them had agreed to have a trial run and to celebrate same in some pub. Celebration over and on the way back to Wickenby when a flat tyre developed. Luckily, outside a garage. No spare so they asked the garage mechanic to put some air in the flat. Which he did. To show its objection, the tyre exploded. This, she explained, was why they were on three tyres only and going at such a slow pace.

At this stage the sergeant said he was on duty shortly so she climbed back in. The Austin continued on its crawl. As I passed them on my bike, I received cheery waves from all four.

**7 August 1944**
'All operational aircrew to report for briefing at 14:00hrs,' ordered the Tannoy. And at our special bomb aimers' pre-briefing at 13:00 the pain that shot into my guts was so fierce I could hardly breathe. Had thought myself pretty well experienced by now, virtually well able to take all that could come. But not when I saw 'Berlin'. The Big City, now referred to as Chop City by some. God, the losses over Berlin! Seem to remember that over four raids at the beginning of the year, 158 kites bought it. A slugging match with masses of night fighters all along the route with even more over Berlin itself: and the heaviest concentration of flak in all Germany. Guy next to me at the pre-briefing mumbles we've had it now, that our chances are virtually nil. And the short walk to the main Briefing Room is more of a despondent shuffle, hardly anybody speaking. Can read what you like in the newspapers about the high morale of our aircrews, but now it had gone through the floor. Mine certainly had and similarly so had that of, I think, every single one of us. Rest of the crews, as we entered, could tell from our faces that it was a nasty one. Confirmed when some of us whispered the target as we sat down. But even although, by then, the target was generally known in the Briefing Room, when the cover of Order of Battle was removed to reveal 'Berlin', an anguished groaning (actually, I think it would be more apt to describe as a kind of despairing moaning) arose all around. Winco Nelson sensibly waited for it to subside. I looked yet again at the long route taking us out over the North Sea, across the Dutch coast then into northern Germany towards Berlin, the Luftwaffe night fighter radio and visual beacons clearly marked on it, and was just about to say something to Vernon when Winco Nelson called for silence. He had just started off on the importance of the Battle of Berlin when a WAAF officer came on to the platform holding what appeared to be a teleprint. She gave it to him. He read it carefully, then looked at us. 'It's scrubbed,' he announced.

A silence at that. But only a brief one as the message sank in. Then cheering: not wild, exciting cheering – more a subdued expression of extreme relief. In war films you see characters displaying stiff upper lips as they go to what, in the film, is certain death. Reckon there had been very few stiff uppers in that Briefing Room until the cancellation teleprint. Certainly mine hadn't been so although I would not have said it was actually quivering. Like everybody else, when Winco Nelson announced the scrubbing, I felt the relief sweep over me: and my stomach was back to normal even before I was aware of it.

Winco Nelson dismissed us but said nobody to go off the station just in case some alternative target came through later (although he didn't think it would). We went to the Mess for a pint.

You can, if you wish, obtain a couple of pills to keep you awake on a long flight. The WOP (Sergeant Dunn) elected to take a couple when we were briefed to undertake the long haul to Berlin: which he did, right there in the Briefing Room. Seems he had decided that his Western novels were not enough to keep his eyes open and that he needed some other stimulant. When Berlin was cancelled and someone remarked upon his taking these pills, he shrugged, said he never had any trouble sleeping and that the pills wouldn't really make any difference once he was in his pit. (Discovered later that, after an hour abed, he got up, dressed, and walked around the airfield till the Sergeants' Mess opened for breakfast!)

| | |
|---|---|
| *Op. No. 28* | *8-9 August 1944* |
| *Target* | Oil storage depot at AIRE SURLYS |
| *A/C 'B'* | (Glad to be back in good old 'B' for Baker once more: nothing went wrong *this* time)<br>*Load* 11 x 1,000lbs.<br>4 x 500lbs. |
| *Take off* | 21:30hrs. *Duration* 3.20hrs. |
| *Height* | 11,000ft. |
| *Flak* | Nil |
| *S/Ls* | A few |
| *E/A* | None sighted. A few believed to have been knocking around, but I for my part didn't witness any interceptions |

Bombing very concentrated. Oil tanks left blazing behind us. The way we, and the Yanks, are going for oil targets suggests Germans must be getting short of it.

Why, despite this easy and comparatively 'gentle' operation, did I find myself full of fear and foreboding? It reminded me of our first ops. Is the reason that, in the beginning, one resigned oneself to the seemingly inescapable fact that this was it, that one would never complete more than a few before buying it? Could be. And now, coming to the end of the tour, one senses just the chance that we might make it? I think that's it. But all I know is that, right now, I'm getting the jitters. So are some of the others.

**Later**

On the above subject, when we got leave in July and I went home I arrived at 05.30 hrs. Rang the front door bell. Immediately my folks' bedroom window jerked open and my mother stuck her head out. She was dreading the telegraph boy. Later, about 08.30, I went down to Portobello to catch Ann, my fiancée, as she boarded the tram for Edinburgh. She turned quite white. Not surprising: there they are every day hearing of Bomber Command's massive losses and visualising me as one of those 'missing, believed killed'.

On that leave I went to visit Mr and Mrs Lees in Bath Street. Wish I hadn't. Their only son, Scott, was my constant companion until the war: he joined up as air-gunner and went missing when on Wellingtons in Egypt. That was about two months ago. When I called I could read in Mr Lees's eyes that I was alive and well and why not Scott? Even sadder when he asked if there was still a chance that Scott could turn up. No use making sympathetic, and meaningless, noises there. Mrs Lees told me that every evening her husband goes into his studio (he is a photographer) and weeps for his son. No, I wish I hadn't gone. Selfish, I know.

And while on this subject, last week I recognised an armourer working on the Lanc as a Portobello fellow. Name of Black. We chatted for a while. As we concluded our conversation, he informed me that, if I were to be shot down, on his next leave he would visit my folk to tell them when and how. Considerate, I suppose, but I'd have preferred him not to be quite so helpful . . .

**9 August 1944**

Having lunch with Horsfall and Vernon when the Chief Intelligence Officer brought in two Fleet Air Arm pilots. They sat down beside us, the CIO introducing the Navy bods. He didn't say why they were here and, of course, we didn't ask. Some talk about radar during which CIO mentioned $H_2S$. I said 'B' for Baker equipped with it and that, now that I was more experienced in its use, I thought it quite terrific. CIO added that if I had nothing on after lunch would I mind taking the two FAA pilots out to the Lanc to show them it. Said I'd be delighted.

It being a very pleasant afternoon, I walked with the pair of them out to the bay where 'B' was parked. On our way we started chatting about the war in general. Somehow the subject of the sinking of 'Prince of Wales' and 'Repulse' cropped up. Was surprised how bitter these two became. Against Admiral Sir Tom Philips: one of the old school, they criticised, who completely under-estimated the power of the air, who simply would not recognise the fact that the day of the big capital ship was over unless provided with full air cover. On my observing that when Philips wanted to sail from Singapore to intercept a reported Japanese invasion fleet, the last remaining Buffalos (obsolete American fighters) were out and could not return in time they said OK, but why on earth didn't he break his wireless silence when spotted by the Jap recce planes? The Buffalos were back by then and, while no match for Jap kites in general, probably would have managed to break up the Jap bombing attacks and thus maybe save the two ships. I had no answer to that, really. Especially when these two went on to maintain that, our air power in the Far East being almost non-existent, the 'Prince of Wales' and 'Repulse' would have been sunk anyway: if not in Singapore then in the Indian Ocean. To add to the general air of despondency on that walk they maintained that while as regards actual seamanship the RN left the Americans standing, when it came to operating flat tops the Yanks were way way ahead. I was countering that with the fact that the RN has to make do with naval adaptations of RAF aircraft while the Americans are able to build ones specifically designed for operating from carriers, when we arrived at the bay. They were most interested in the $H_2S$. Also so interested in 'B' for Baker that they spent the best part of an hour clambering over her and asking questions. Think that, had they been given the opportunity, they would have transferred to 12 Squadron there and then!

**Later (early evening)**

Just been reading a most interesting article in today's paper. In commenting on the lack of Luftwaffe activity against us (and our land forces) in France, I had always reckoned this being due to so much of the Luftwaffe being switched to the Eastern Front, but this Air Correspondent has a completely different theory. He maintains that the German Air Force is facing today a terrible dilemma exactly similar to that faced by the RAF in 1940 during the Battle of France: it has to decide whether to commit its full strength into supporting the German armies in France – and in so doing incurring massive losses – or to hold it back for the defence of the Reich itself. Like the RAF in France in 1940 it cannot do both. And, of course, the Luftwaffe will have learned the lesson of the RAF: namely that had we flung nearly all our fighters into that absolutely hopeless preliminary Battle of France (as the French wanted us to do) we would have lost the Battle of Britain. Yes, I think this Air Correspondent has the right gen there. It certainly fits in with the fact that on our ops over France we don't encounter all that much opposition while over Germany it's the exact opposite. He more or less proves his theory when he points out that it was in the strongest Luftwaffe airfield concentration area in Europe that the Allied landings took place: and that this had been constructed on the same basis as the RAF's earlier strategy – namely successive circles of airfields planned to allow for retreat. OK, but if Herman changes his mind and decides to fight it out over France he'll delight hundreds of bods in their Spits, Mustangs, Mosquitos, Thunderbolts, Typhoons, etc. Won't delight us in the Lancs all that much. Unless the fighter boys do all their stuff first . . .

A forecast alongside this article that the price of fags might go up again. Hope not; they're dear enough as it is 20 Capstan, and similar, rising to 2/4d as against the bob they were when the war started. Not 2/4d in the Mess, though, or in the NAAFI: there you get them for 1/6d although you don't always manage to obtain the brand you want. Sometimes buy my stepfather Erinmore tobacco in the Mess and post it on to him. It's sometimes in very short supply in civvy street and he smokes nothing else.

While I'm reading the paper someone turns on the radio and starts fiddling with the dial. He obtains a new station which went on the air in early June: the BBC Allied Expeditionary Forces Programme beamed towards France. (But reception here seems good.) BBC must reckon they've got a lot of Yanks in their audience because they play two Shaw records in succession – 'Day in, day out', and 'My Heart Stood Still'. The character at the radiogram observes that his effing heart is always standing still these days and switches the set off.

**9 August 1944**

Odd, sometimes, how one just suddenly stops and takes stock. Of life, I mean. And when you do that you start having a look back along Memory lane which, to me, is a pretty busy thoroughfare.

Don't know how far back along it I want to go, though. Certainly not to my childhood days which I remember as boring: of all pre-war recollections boredom seems to come through the strongest. (As for that terrible Scots Sunday, the only praying I ever did was for Monday to hurry along.) I think the boredom began to evaporate when Hitler marched into Poland and I began to realise that an escape route was presenting itself. And it did. From the moment I joined the RAF, boredom became a thing of the past. One was free. From day-to-day office routine: from going to night-school to try to obtain a bit of paper. And, most of all, from one's parents. The discipline of the RAF was, in effect, a form of freedom when, once off duty, you didn't really need to account to anybody for your movements. To stay out all night, all that was required was a Sleeping Out Pass and on your return no need to explain where you'd been and what you'd done. True, only two bob a day pay, but you seemed to get by on it. Sounds a small enough matter now when sitting here at Wickenby writing it down, but at the time represented a massive breakthrough into the life which was going on all around you and which you were missing.

And all those interesting people you were flung up against. Even that Blackpool landlady on whom we were billeted and who had two standards of meals – one for 'paying guests' and one for us – fascinating. 'Yes, you can have a bath, son; just give us tuppence for the coal.' Had a smashing daughter who made eyes at us all and who displayed lots of leg when seated. Dated her, but nothing doing. The rest of the billettees had her down as a 'prick teaser'; it was the first time I learned the true meaning of the description. On this subject, the Corporal in charge of our squad used to march us now and then to Derby Street baths. Most did not bother with swimming pants: the female attendants, from the gallery, spent much time in nodding admiration of various bods who strutted around the sides of the pool but never actually entered it.

Next to Martlesham Heath and Bawdsey. Then, at long last, via Regents Park, London, to St. Andrews for the start of the aircrew training which was to conclude with my arriving here at 12 Squadron, No. 1 Group, RAF Bomber Command.

But at that time (October 1941) the likelihood of flying in any aircraft, far less the Lancaster, was a long way away. (Had never been up anyway and often wondered if I'd be sick: also whether I'd be scared. Felt I'd probably be both.)

By now all pre-war boredom completely forgotten. Was able to hold my own with the others, not being quite so green, having to fend more for myself. Also by now able to avoid authority without appearing to be against it.

January 1942, and off to Heaton Park, Manchester, HM Transport to Canada, Moncton, New Brunswick, followed by a delightful train journey to Arizona. God, I could hardly believe it! Before the war, practically my only excursion from Edinburgh had been to London and now here I was in the Wild West. Even managed a trip to Los Angeles and Hollywood from the RAF station at Mesa, near Phoenix. Never for a moment dreamed when I used to watch those Hollywood epics at the Portobello cinemas that one day I'd be in the place itself. Impressed? I was more than just impressed! To be honest with myself, I don't think I was capable of taking it all in.

There was, of course, the little matter of flying. Wasn't sick on that very first flight. Was scared; but not as much as I'd thought I'd be.

As well as my first time in the air, Arizona also saw my first time in another field. In the back of a Chevrolet, to be exact. And if anybody was entitled to yell 'rape' it certainly wasn't her. After that, she was waiting for me at the camp gates in that Chevrolet most evenings: sometimes we stayed in the Chevvy and sometimes I managed to find two bucks for a room in the Adam Hotel in Phoenix. (She wanted to pay, but no dice.) Rather liked that girl: maybe the fact that I was heading for 21 and would have reached that age still virginal had it not been for her had something to do with it.

Eliminated from pilot training shortly after. No connection with the Chevvy or the room at the Adam – my co-ordination was shocking.

Sorry, though, to have to leave that flying field at Mesa. Run by the RAF with civvy instructors. Practically no bull, the RAF letting it be known that the only time they'd clamp down on us would be if we ran foul of the local police, got drunk, did anything to sour Anglo-American relations and, above all, criticised any of the recruits from a nearby US Army training camp who looked as if they couldn't have fought their way out of a paper bag. As far as I know, the RAF didn't have to clamp down on anybody on these accounts. They did take action, however – or so I was told – on one cadet who caught a dose of the clap (there was a lot of it about). Sent him back to Canada.

Which was to where I now returned. And after being held at RCAF Trenton, in Ontario, went off to Paulson, Manitoba, to do my Bombing and Gunnery course. But beginning to become worried; now July 1942 and the war might be over before I can get back to England and fly operationally. Navigation training at Winnipeg took up another two months and worries disappeared when I was awarded my half-wing. Then complete disaster: had been unwise enough to come top of the course so had to remain in Canada to instruct. Refused my commission, threatened all kinds of disobedience and insubordination, but to no avail; they'd heard it all before. Had matured somewhat, however, and came *bottom* of the Instructors' Course at Mountainview: was also a very indifferent instructor when returned to Paulson. Which must have helped, because by July 1943 I was on the boat again.

Had come a long way since September 1940. Was now getting nearer Wickenby here; although, naturally, at the time I didn't know it would be Wickenby – didn't even know if it would be Lancs. But that was me heading for Operational training (of which I've recorded some bits and pieces earlier on). When I reflect on the cost, not only financially but in man-hours and material, of training me just to get to this stage, together with the cost of operational training still to be incurred, I think maybe Horsfall's attitude over the guy who was stripped of wings and rank at that parade we had to attend when we first arrived here was the only one.

This entry has turned out to be a resumé of my RAF career to date. Didn't intend it to, but it has. Should confine myself to the present rather than the past. And the most vital aspect of the present is that we've got only two more operational flights to do. Maybe it would be more apt to observe that we *still have* two more to do. Could end on either. Been writing for too long tonight and am tired: it's now 3 am and think I should get back into bed and try to get some sleep. But I'll put down what's in my mind and if, when I read it after breakfast, I feel it's maudlin, or even plain daft, I'll do something I've never done since I started this diary – I'll delete it. It's this: when I think back on how utterly boring life was before the war and compare it with what I've had out of the RAF, from the day I joined it, in way of experience, travel, comradeship, exhileration – even fear – well, if the worst comes to the worst, somehow or another I cannot feel I will have lost out.

**Added after breakfast**

Yes, it *is* maudlin: and plain daft to boot. (And I didn't even have a half-pint!) But I can't bring myself to delete it. Don't suppose it matters whether I do or don't.

**10 August 1944**

Was asked this morning, by a bod who'd just arrived, if they had many parades here at Wickenby. On being questioned as to his interest he replied that parades got him down, that he made a point of missing them. Told him we'd been on only one parade here and that was the disheartening effort where the NCO was stripped of his wings and tapes. Said he would have skipped that one particularly.

But there are no parades here as far as I am aware. Certainly not for us: and, I'm quite sure, not for the airmen. About the nearest thing to a parade I've seen at Wickenby has been a squad of WAAFs doing some drill under an NCO and being supervised by the Queen Bee. Learned that that was some disciplinary measure – a form of punishment for doing, or not doing, God knows what. Funny, but the WAAF officers seem to exert a firmer discipline over their airwomen than we do over the airmen. Maybe should qualify that by adding that aircrew officers as a rule *don't* exert any discipline over *anybody*. Not here, anyway. I suppose that if walking past SHQ and an airman doesn't cock you one up you'd stop him and reprimand him. But that probably only in case some senior officer happened to be looking out of the window. In any case, while the ground staff don't salute and 'sir' out at the Lanc, I don't think any of them would be stupid enough to walk past you in front of SHQ without giving you a salute. Or something which passed for same.

| | |
|---|---|
| *Op. No. 29* | *10-11 August 1944* |
| *Target* | Mining in the GIRONDE area (CORDOVAN) |
| *A/C 'A'* | (Can't have 'B' for Baker as she's on 50 hour inspection. *Must* have her for our next – and last – op. Must have her – oh, Christ, we must!) |
| *Load* | 6x1,500lb. Sea Mines |
| *Take off* | 21:15hrs. *Duration* 6.45hrs. |
| *Height* | 5,000ft. |
| *Flak* | Some light guns |
| *S/Ls* | Just one or two |
| *E/A* | Saw a couple. Looked like JU88's. But no attacks made on us: just as well as it was a clear, cloudless sky |

Only eight a/c on this boring effort. Not much excitement in flying 3 hours there and 3 hours back just to drop six bloody sea mines. The code name for this kind of operating is: 'Gardening'. One missing (F/L Owens): believed hit by flak and crashed in England.

Nearing the dropping area when Dunn announced he was getting Artie Shaw on his radio (he knows I'm a Shavian fanatic) and would he put him on? I said yes and nobody said no so on came Shaw over the intercom playing 'Rose Room'. Not at his most mellifluous, but good solid swing. Next – no announcements from this station – we got 'Donkey Serenade': and the mines went down to the accompaniment of 'Copenhagen', the last-named evoking the hope expressed by Horsfall that we'd never have to bomb the bloody place.

All this much against the rules of the game: Dunn should have been on listening watch and we should have been on the lookout, not enjoying the relaxing effect of swing music. Don't know where that station was: maybe Bordeaux, or maybe even Spain. Certainly came in clear and loud. Billie Holiday had just started on 'Any Old Time' when Vernon said he was fed up with Shaw and could Dunn not get Glenn Miller? At which stage this station went off the air . . .

Just one more to go. On reflection, I shouldn't have moaned about this mining effort because I reckon all of us would give a hell of a lot to have our final op as easy as that. Yes, that's it: the last one and it's all over.

**12 August 1944**

The Tannoy has just ordered all operational air crews to report to the Briefing Room at 16.00 hrs. The navigators' and bomb aimers' pre-briefing is slightly in advance. Am writing this before I go. Afraid my hand is trembing slightly. Dreading the target simply because it's the last target of the tour. And yet, maybe I shouldn't be panicking as I am; this last, this final, target could well turn out to be some piece of cake over France. Still, quite a few of the French raids have been dicey enough. Well, I'll know quite soon now. It's 15.30 so in less that 30 minutes we'll learn the target. But wish it was over. The operation, I mean. Now, if it only could be about 8 o'clock tomorrow morning then I would have it all behind me. One way or another.

| | |
|---|---|
| *Op. No. 30* | *12-13 August 1944* |
| *Target* | BRUNSWICK – city flattening |
| *A/C 'B'* | (A prayer answered – we had beloved 'B' for Baker for the last one) |
| *Load* | 1 x 2,000lbs.<br>12 x J-type incendiary clusters |
| *Take off* | 21:30hrs. *Duration* 5.25hrs. |
| *Height* | 19,000ft. |

Am able to give this last one the full treatment because I have the time to do so. Lots of time, really, because it's not a question of completing your tour the one night and being away from here the following day.

That was it; the last one. And the last time I'll be recording that pain in the guts when I learned the target (seems I've been noting that down quite often: wonder if other bods experience it – or that it's merely the fact I was more cowardly). But Brunswick for our final one: and with it the conviction that it's final in every way. Twenty-nine ops, only four of them being over the Reich, and we end up with a bastard target like this. The seven of us sit there in the Briefing Room looking glum, not speaking, trying to take in what was being said: maybe the others, like myself, reflecting just our hellish luck not to finish with a comparatively easy French effort.

The silence is broken when briefing over. All start snarling away. At the RAF, at 'Butch' for being so dedicated to destroying German cities, at each other. Particularly the latter, our language worse than ever before. None of us exactly twitching, but not very far off it. Some frantic smoking on the way out to the bay and before we climb aboard. Plus more snarling and cursing.

Take off not as clever as usual: so much petrol and such a heavy bomb load, Vernon has to fight like hell to get her airborne. A slow climb for height then on course for the Dutch coast.

And there the flak's coming up giving the appearance of coloured, twinkling, confetti in reverse. Bursting all around us, the shrapnel sounding like hailstones as it hits the fuselage. And it's not a case of getting through it and into the clear; there's flak inland too – heavy, concentrated stuff, well predicted. Then cone after cone of searchlights. Are trapped ourselves by one. Christ, it's like suddenly finding yourself naked in front of thousands of people. Violent corkscrewing – really headlong stuff which brings the sour taste of vomit to your mouth – before we manage to get free. During the manoeuvre catch a glimpse of another Lanc being held by a cone. Why isn't he corkscrewing? Then lose sight.

Now time for me to start slinging out the window (bundles of thick paper strips black one side, silver on the other and cut to a specific length). This to upset German radar. Which it does: all the S/Ls become stationary for a while before evidently going on to manual and the predicted flak tails off. One or two of the S/Ls remain pointing almost vertically upwards and I catch sight of a ME110 below us flying through the beam of one. Maybe only momentarily but long enough for me to see the German crosses on the wings. So that's the night fighters on the scene, probably vectored here from every available base. A sudden flurry of tracer underneath us and to port signals an interception: shortly after, another eruption of tracer – much nearer us this time – but can't see whether or not the fighter's made a kill because Cartwright is yelling, 'corkscrew, corkscrew' and we're in an acute dive to starboard.

Flying level again and my windowing over, I climb into the front turret. Quite a view! From above us a constant flow of flares to guide the fighters is being dropped very accurately all along the bomber stream (no doubt by older aircraft). As I cock the Brownings, one of the flares bursts ahead slightly to port and in its light I see an ME110 almost level with us. I yell 'corkscrew, corkscrew, corkscrew' – hysterically, I think – and as Vernon dives headlong to starboard I fire my guns at the ME110. I'm convinced this is a night fighter come-hither, the tactics being for No. 1 to fly level with the bomber, just near enough to be spotted then, while the crew of the latter are straining away to identify him, No. 2 creeps up on the Lanc's tail and that's the end of the matter as far as *that* particular bomber is concerned. Remain convinced of this tactic despite our experts saying a co-ordinated effort like that between two fighters is simply not possible. Level again and back at 19,000 feet, I see more interceptions and two of our kites going down. Shouldn't stop my own searching, but find my eyes drawn to the dreadful sight of two bombers, flames streaking aft, describe graceful curves earthwards at a seemingly slow pace. My eyes keep on them, but I don't see them hit the deck. Hope the crews managed to bale out.

Nearing Brunswick now, so time I got out of the turret and down into my bombing compartment. Tell Vernon I'm doing so and have just unplugged my intercom when there's a stream of tracer flying past us. Another violent corkscrewing while I'm trying to make my compartment.

Everything ready and Brunswick coming up. A fearsome barrage of flak, set to our height, on the approach. So thick you wonder if there's possibly one bit of the sky ahead that could be free of it. You know you've got to fly into it and through it and (sounds so bloody dramatic as I sit here writing!) you say to yourself that this is the chop. On your very last one and where has your effing luck gone?

Can smell the cordite from the bursts all around us. There's also the rattle of the shrapnel hitting us; it just seems to go on and on. Like being in a greenhouse during a prolonged hail-storm. Louder noises suggest we've been hit more severely, but the bomb-doors are open and we're on the bombing run now. This is what we came for and I must get it right. Have to give Vernon only two slight corrections and I have the aiming point sliding up smoothly. It hits the graticule and I press the tit. Down goes the heavy boy and the clusters of incendiaries. Into what, even from 19,000 feet, seems a furnace of swirling, angry flame. Order the bomb-bay doors to be closed and at the same time wonder if anybody can be alive down there. Stop wondering when, on Cartwright's yell, we're off corkscrewing again. Have to wait until we've ditched the fighter before opening the panel to check no bombs still hanging up. If there were, the Germans would get them, not the Dutch. But all OK.

On to turning point beyond the target then starting on homeward journey. Flak still tearing at us but now not quite so heavy. But more fighter flares. I see from the front turret quite a number of interceptions. At least one of them is a kill because a bomber explodes in mid-air. More flak and S/Ls on way towards the Dutch coast. Flak just as heavy there as on our way in. Night fighters still after us and more interceptions: they even follow us out to sea.

Eventually, after what seems ages, the English coast. Some humour around now: suddenly everbody loves everybody. Jesus Christ! We've made it. We've done the thirty even although the last was a bastard like Brunswick. No thought of the number of people we must have killed. God, with the sky over Brunswick virtually crowded with bombers the death roll must be massive. But Hitler should have thought about retaliation when he started the war.

Yes, over now. Only got to land safely and that's it.

But it isn't quite. Making our approach to the runway and, suddenly, a Lanc ahead of us erupting. We get the code word. It's 'Intruders'. (JU88s: no bombs, just loaded with cannon.) They slip into the returning bomber stream, accompany the Lancs returning to base and into the circuit then wait until one of them is landing and thus a sitting duck. Climb to a certain height, fly northwards on a certain course, the theory being that any aircraft not doing so is enemy and can therefore be shot down. (But what about any of our *own* who, through damage, don't receive the secret signal?) Not so sure it was Intruders anyway – there haven't been any around for ages. Maybe simply a badly damaged Lanc exploding on landing and Control understandably playing it safe. In any event, we are recalled after about 15 minutes and land safely.

Winco Nelson's there when we climb out of 'B' for Baker. Has beer for us in his car. Never did beer taste as good as that bottle I had. Wonder if the Winco greets with a bottle of beer all his crews who complete a tour. Asks us what it was like. Vernon says 'hellish' which is about the mildest expletive I think we've used since yesterday's briefing. We all thereafter, clutching our bottles of beer, go round the Lanc examining the holes. Not as much damage as I had expected: a host of smallish holes plus two or three rather big tears. Winco says she'll be operational again by tomorrow. He then tells us that a special outfit of Lancasters called 'Tiger Force' is to be formed to go to the Far East to bomb Japan and would we like, as a crew, to volunteer? He takes no offence to the rude reply to this: especially as the word 'sir' is affixed to it. He grins and says, 'the Japs cut these off only for starters'. After he goes off, and while we're awaiting the transport, I pat 'B' for Baker and whisper thanks to her for being so perfect, so faithful, so wonderful. But I'm careful not to let any of the others see or hear me doing this otherwise they'd think I really *have* gone round the bend.

Have now ascertained that on Saturday night more than 1,300 tons were dropped on Brunswick by 400 bombers in exactly 15 minutes. Bomber Command had more than 1,300 aircraft out over a 24 hour period on raids which included Keil, Frankfurt, flying-bomb sites in northern France, plus mine laying. We have 48 of our planes missing including two from Wickenby. That's 343 of the boys, assuming all the aircraft were Lancs. Not all killed, but, even so, rather heavy losses.

Total operational hours 149.35.

Reflecting that we got off lightly on that tour, though. Especially compared with aircrews who embarked on their tours as little as a year ago. Then nearly every op was over Germany bringing with it, in practically all cases, heavy losses. When we arrived here at Wickenby it was those losses we had in mind. Which, really, is why I was so pessimistic when I started this diary. Didn't for a moment dream that in the event we would do only five over the Reich and the other twenty-five over Occupied Europe. True, losses there also, but on nowhere the same scale as those incurred by Bomber Command over Germany. Have the Invasion to thank for that: and, of course, the run-up to it. Would think that, once the Allied Armies advance enough to be able to do without the services of the heavies, 'Butch' will get them all back again and will resume his dedicated task of flattening Germany. If he does, our tour has been just at the most opportune time – a comparatively easy one sandwiched between those earlier heavy losses and those which are certainly still to come when the nasty stuff is resumed. Hope I enjoy as much good luck for the remainder of the war.

Have almost a feeling of anti-climax as I await posting away from here. It's all over, but I feel something has gone out of my life. Missing the excitement, I suppose. Spoke to Vernon and Horsfall about it. Seems they feel rather the same. I asked Vernon if, now that he was going off to the USAAF, whether he would volunteer for Flying Fortress ops. He said like a pig's ass he would, that he'd done his thirty with the RAF and that was that. But I don't know: there was some kind of a gleam in his eye, although only fleeting. He asked me if I'd volunteer for a second tour. I replied no dice: and meant it. Horsfall also said no dice, but he's daft over machine guns and almost in the same breath mentioned the possibility of Lancs now being equipped with .5s. So while his no dice is probably meant just now I wouldn't be surprised if sooner or later he's on a second tour. If he can get himself on to one, that is: there is now a surplus of trained aircrew all awaiting operational flying and it may become policy to use them rather than the older hands.

Maybe some of this anti-climax is due to the fact that we see the Lancs taking off on ops, know that we're no longer part of the force – we don't even know their targets – and feel rather out of things. Will fade as soon as we leave here, I think.

Bump into the Mess Secretary today who, after informing me of his delight at the prospect of my early departure from Wickenby, warns me darkly to be sure to pay my Mess Bill before I take off: and almost in the same breath adds that he supposes I'll want a bottle of whisky to shove into my case. At cost price too. When I nod that I was rather banking on it he says maybe he'll rise to a couple, he's so pleased to see the back of me: also to make sure I have a pint with him tonight. Will miss him. Will also miss quite a few of the other bods around here. Especially, I think, Winco Nelson who I'd like to meet up with again somewhere or another. Things don't often work out that way in the RAF, though: probably will never see him again.

**15 August 1944**

Nearly asked for it today. Our final op was 12-13 August, but we are hanging around here awaiting posting which, we are told, won't be through for a day or two yet. So walked out to the bay where 'B' for Baker was parked. Just to have yet another look at her. Maybe even to bid her farewell yet again. Stupid, really, to become so attached to an aircraft: I'll be glad when I'm away from Wickenby and it'll be impossible for me to see her. Another crew climbing all over. I feel resentful: she's ours, not theirs. And will they take good care of her, anyway? The pilot, whom I know by sight, informs me that they've just been given her for their very own. I ask how many they've done. He says fourteen so I don't feel so bad: they'll be an experienced enough crew to stand a good chance of not losing her in a hurry. He adds that he's going up on an air test that afternoon: and lets it slip that his bomb aimer and mid-upper won't be going along because of some other duty. I can come for the ride, if I like. Was sorely tempted. But that simply would have been asking for it. Had done the thirty and to fly from Wickenby on an air test purely on sentimental grounds would have been asking for it, despite the fact that 'B' for Baker's new 'owners' had fourteen behind them. So I said no thanks.

Watched the take-off in the afternoon, however. Seemed smooth and expert enough.

Last I saw of her.

**16 August 1944**

That bugger Lord Haw-Haw again with his sneering drawl, 'Jairmany calling, Jairmany calling'. Then telling us that our raids on the Reich are doing practically no damage, not hindering the German war effort one little bit, but are killing innocent women and children. Different when the Luftwaffe laid waste to Rotterdam: different to 1937 when the same Luftwaffe, during the Spanish Civil War, made a mass aerial attack on Guernica, the ancient Basque cultural capital, in order to gain experience for the forthcoming world war. I do hope they can catch that traitor when it's over. But pretty certain they won't – he'll manage to get away to Argentina or some other South American state.

After writing this, departed to the Mess in something of a bad mood and immediately became involved in an argument with an Education Officer. (Why are so many of these types such red-hot socialists?) A school teacher and like so many school teachers – but certainly not all – thought he knew everything. Wonder what it is about school teachers. Is it because so many of them leave school, go to University or Training College then back to school again without having any idea of what's going on in the great big world outside? Anyway, and maybe it's my fault really because I was in a rotten mood when I got to the Mess, we established a relationship akin to a pork butcher putting to a rabbi his intention of setting up a stall in his synagogue. Over one of my pet hates – disarmament. This guy's conviction was that after the war we should disarm and that, when we did so, everybody else would follow and it would be peace, perfect peace. For him, no learning from the lessons of history that our disarmament policies of the 1920s and 1930s helped to bring about this Second World War, that, with the government refusing to finance the development of monoplane fighters, it was only foresight, and patriotism, of Lady Houston, Rolls-Royce, Vickers and Hawker-Siddeley, that enabled the Hurricane and Spitfire to be developed in time to save us in the Battle of Britain.

No, he just didn't want to know, waving aside any assumption that Hitler started this war convinced that Britain was too weak and decadent to oppose him, that it could well have been a different story had we been strong and powerful.

Trouble is that after the war people like him will return to teaching and impress young minds with all his dangerous theories about disarmament.

We did not part on the best of terms.

**19 August 1944**

Our last night on 12 Squadron and Vernon, Horsfall and myself agreed to meet in the bar about eight. There being nothing on, quite a few other bods turned up; some, according to Horsfall, just for a free drink, but most either to take part in a booze-up or simply to join us in a farewell party. Had to pay cash, of course, our Mess bills now being settled and our bar accounts closed. So we each put a fiver into a kitty, left it on the bar and bought pints for all who came up to it, non-flying types included. There are a lot of pints in fifteen quid so by ten o'clock there was a certain amount of merriment in the air. Winco Nelso came in, wouldn't accept a drink out of our kitty, but bought us one. Stayed long enough for a brief chat then wished us well reminding me, on leaving, not to forget my bike. The Mess Secretary looked in, had a pint on us, then took off after expressing the hope that he wouldn't find his ante-room wrecked in the morning. A needless worry because there were no games last night, not even singing: it stayed simply as a convivial drinking and nattering session. Chief conversation was, naturally, ops, one or two expressing surprise and envy, I think, that we'd managed to get through the thirty in as short a space of time as approximately eleven weeks. Which we had done thanks mainly to the lead up to the Invasion and, of course, the Invasion itself. Some sprog crews joined in, although diffidently at first: one newly arrived pilot, after a few pints, asked what we felt had been the greatest contributing factor to our surviving the thirty and, after admitting we'd had an easy tour, I told him corkscrewing. At which Horsfall advised an air-gunner standing beside him to yell 'corkscrew' even if the speck on his turret window turned out to be fly shit. No line shooting. Didn't feel like it and it wouldn't have gone down well anyway. Keep the line-shooting for the civvies!

The C of E devil dodger came in, had a pint from us which he seemed to enjoy thoroughly. He listended to the chat but really took no part in it. Especially as no-one mentioned religion and, I think, would have taken exception had the padre tried to introduce the subject. He was just finishing his pint when someone shoved on a record of Shaw's 'Stardust' at full throttle. He grimaced when the strident trumpet solo reverberated round the ante-room, made some excuse about having work to do, drained his glass, wished us all the best, and left.

With the padre gone, the discussion switched suddenly from ops to which, in that ante-room anyway, seemed to be the only alternative. Some boasting about prowess made greater as the result of a pint or two. Our fifteen quid was by now becoming extinguished and everybody had had as much as he wanted, or could take, so even the stories of sexual exploits, real or imagined, began to tail off. One by one bods drifted away from the bar until only the three of us were left. So we finished our pints, indicated to the bar steward that we didn't want the odd quid remaining, and left.

Woke with something of a hangover this morning. Packed after breakfast, being especially careful with the two bottles of whisky I'd got from the Mess Secretary – break my heart if, at 14/- each, they got broken! Then sat around waiting for the transport. The seven of us in it and just at the guardhouse when I realised I'd left it behind. My bike. Transport had to turn round and go back for it. So much bad language directed at me by all the crew that I almost felt we were back together in 'B' for Baker . . .

**20 August 1944**

Concluding this diary on way to Edinburgh, the train being hauled by 'Mallard' – still going strong despite being about eight years old. (Certainly knew how to build locomotives at those Doncaster workshops.) Can't really say why I started on it: have kept a diary only once before, and even that was only a spasmodic, occasional jotting down of experiences in Canada and America. Maybe maintained these scrawlings as a kind of therapeutic exercise although not particularly aware of it at the time – I simply don't know. Just been glancing back over the pages and been grimacing over the number of split infinitives, changes in tenses for no apparent reason, even rank bad English. Wouldn't dare show it to 'Chinkie' Westwood, my former English master at Heriot's: he'd be well launched into a session of the havering hab-dabs when less than half-way through it! Not going to show it to *anybody,* when it comes to that.

Said cheers and all the best to Vernon, Horsfall, Norman, Griggs, Dunn and Cartwright. Understand that many crews – now, like us, designated 'ex-operational' – intend trying to keep in touch and accordingly exchange addresses. But these would be crews which became involved during the tour in much closer relationships than we did: crews which went to pubs together. All despite the fact that maybe only the pilot (sometimes maybe one other) was commissioned.

But close rapport was never our lot. When I recorded brief notes on the other six of the crew half-way through the tour I had thought that this might develop eventually. True, we all got around to using Christian names but that was about as far as 'closeness' went. Wasn't a question of rank, either; Vernon, Horsfall or myself never pulled that on any of the Sergeants. Think, basically, that the fact that each of us had different interests, different outlooks, and sometimes different standards, kept us from gelling. But, as I noted at the time also, we flew well together as a crew, which was the main thing by far: indeed, the *only* thing.

There was no sorrow at the breaking up of us as a crew. No attempt to exchange addresses. And I go along with that: no useful purpose in it, really. That, incidentally, is one of the differences between us and the Army.

In the latter you (usually) meet some guy at the Recruit Centre with whom immediately you hit it off: and (usually) you serve together for quite a time, in some cases for a very long time, thereby establishing a bond. A purpose in keeping up a friendship established like that. But in the RAF usually you are posted somewhere-or-another on your own. True, there are exceptions, but it usually works out that way. You're friendly with some particular bod for a while: then it's another bod somewhere else; and so on.

No, no useful purpose in exchanging addresses. Also no useful purpose in telling each other where posted. In the event, mine came first. After leave. A month it is. Always said I'd wait until the war's over before getting married. Most sensible idea, that: after all, I could be ordered on to a second tour of 30 (although that's unlikely: the RAF now have more trained aircrew than they know what to do with): then the Japs don't look like being anywhere near the end of their tether, so I could end up in the Far East. Yes, better to wait. But all the same . . . all the same. Have to discuss it with Ann: see if her views have changed now I'm over my ops.

Meantime, after the leave, my posting. To Andreas in the Isle of Man. Yet one more item which makes me grateful to the RAF – another area which, before the war, I had never visualised visiting.

Got a bone to pick with them when I arrive there, however. I'm an experienced, ex-operational bomb aimer, have some solo, if admittedly third-rate, pilot hours to my credit; and was informed, orally, that I was going to Andreas as a bombing instructor. The posting notice has me down as M.T. Officer. Well, at least by the time I've sorted it out they'll have taught me to *drive* . . .

And with Waverley coming up in about ten minutes I can now do what, starting back in May, I was pretty certain I was never going to be able to do.

Which is to stab five stars across the bottom of this notebook. And close it.

**Later**

Opened this diary again to record award of French Croix de Guerre with Silver Star. This to me because, as I learned, 12 Squadron had extinguished its allocation of DFCs. Ah well, at least I got a kiss with mine. From a French General . . .

As I raked out the diary for the above entry, I can't resist a quick glancing over it. Really hard to believe that we took off on that first op on Tergnier at the end of May and that this is now only November. Thirty operational bombings between 1 June and 13 August. Must be a record for a quick tour, that. Hours flown on Lancs were 187.10: but the prologue to that Lanc flying is really 53.04 hrs. on PT 17A (Stearman), 29.40 in Battles, 102.35 in Ansons, 8.30 in Bolingbrokes, 52.25 in Wellingtons, 40.10 in Halifaxes: and, of all things, 30 minutes in a Lysander. Total flying hours *472.04*.

11-08-95

1 *4.95
*4.95 ST
*10.00 AT
*5.05 CG

D 8955